Letters of Light

Bill Gray's home at 14 Bennington Street, Cheltenham. The building is now a cake shop.

Letters of Light

The Magical Letters of William G. Gray to Alan Richardson

SKYLIGHT PRESS

First published in Great Britain in 2015 by Skylight Press,
210 Brooklyn Road, Cheltenham, Glos GL51 8EA

Designed and typeset by Rebsie Fairholm
Publisher: Daniel Staniforth
Cover photo from *The Rollright Ritual*. Incorporating stock texture from sirius-sdz.deviantart.com

www.skylightpress.co.uk

Printed and bound in Great Britain by Lightning Source, Milton Keynes. Typeset in Agmena Pro.

British Library Cataloguing-in-Publication data:
A catalogue record for this book is available from the British Library.

ISBN 978-1-910098-01-1

Introduction

I was 17 when I wrote my first letter to William G. Gray. He was not my only correspondent, even at that age. I have earlier letters from a wide variety of unusual people ranging from the wonderful rogue Lobsang Rampa through to W.E. Butler (who sent me a signed copy of his little book *Magic – its Ritual, Power and Purpose*), the up-and-coming Gareth Knight – plus a host of others whose names have either become legends in the magical/mystical fields or have long since been lost to history. But it was Gray who showed the most interest and gave me the most encouragement. He always replied within 24 hours, and *always* used a first-class stamp. Anything less would have been an insult to the Magic.

As I browsed through my Gravian collection for the first time in many years I found, somehow tucked away among his earliest letters, one from Kenneth Grant. I had written to Grant quoting a piece from the *Book of Law* which assured me that I could demand initiation into the O.T.O.[1] He disagreed, and suggested I might want to do some Work first, by keeping a diary for a full nine months. I was miffed by this, and the idea that he could be so cavalier with his interpretation of the sublime but unfathomable *Liber Al vel Legis* as the cognoscenti called it (of which I was obviously one). Hell, I had already taken my own Unreserved Dedication before the bedroom mirror when I was 15, astrally projected several times, knew the Divine Names of the Sephiroth (even if I did intone them with a broad Geordie accent) and was disappointed that this callow Frater Aossic, as he called himself, couldn't intuit this.

I was 17, omniscient, quietly obnoxious. I knew everything; I knew nothing. I *really* needed putting in my place. And I couldn't have picked anyone better to do this than Bill Gray.

Despite the millions of words that must have comprised his output, he remained a two-fingered typist throughout his life.

---

1   Ordo Templi Orientis

It is only re-reading his letters now that I begin to appreciate how much time, care and effort he devoted to passing on his knowledge. Whatever his faults – and he had many – he never stinted on this. In many ways, through his correspondence, I saw the very best of the man.

Of course in saying that, I am speaking to those who have 'ears to hear and eyes to see'. That is to say, his legendary racism did not crop up at all, and the whole complicated question has been dealt with at some length in my co-written biography of the man, entitled *The Old Sod*.[2] I have seen the book signed to him by the great African shaman and healer Credo Mutwa, with whom he got on wonderfully. I also spoke to someone who had been present in South Africa when Bill lambasted the white shop-owner for his disgusting rudeness to a black customer. To Bill, this was the black man's country, and the whites were intruders. Plus I will labour to point out that my first wife was Chinese and I have many close friends of all races and sexual orientations; I don't think even my worst enemy could accuse me of being racist, sexist or homophobic.

I simply ask people to assess Gray in terms of the following letters, and put aside what they may have plucked from a less-than-accurate holier-than-thou, insufferably superior but dried-up grapevine. Without intending to create any kind of awkward pun, when it comes to William G. Gray, things are never as black and white as they might first appear.

Before my first letter reached him, I had already read his *Ladder of Lights*, and had bought it from the bird-like and red bow-tied Geoffrey Watkins himself in Watkins Bookshop, Cecil Court, London, where I escaped to during a school trip. He told me tales of his own father and Madam Blavatsky, and the spirit bells that rang wherever she walked. He was amused by my pronunciation of Jung with a hard 'j', and had great difficulty with my thick accent but saw my thirst for knowledge. I asked for Gray's book; he tried to persuade me to buy tomes by Raynor Johnson, Joel Goldsmith or even Idries Shah, and said he had heard Gray was a very bad-tempered man. I didn't care. It was hot, mad Western Magic I craved, not cold and drippy Eastern Mysticism. But his last words as I tucked the book away, hiding it

---

2   *The Old Sod* by Alan Richardson and Marcus Claridge. Skylight Press

from the scorn of my school mates, were: "Please accept my good wishes for this most important of all journeys."

Until I began this present volume I had not looked at most of Gray's letters in over 40 years. Today, while I was not surprised by how much of the content I had forgotten, I was startled and touched by the sheer depth and humanity of his replies, even though they were expressed in a completely unsentimental way.

Yet while his Magical knowledge was unsurpassed there was something oddly innocent about the man, and his insight into the outer world at that time was often surprisingly awry. It would be easy to laugh, now, at his comments in 1970 about the Teacher Training colleges as vehicles of sinister government mind-control. In that aspect of life he was totally wrong. In fact they were staffed by failed teachers who could not cope with the firing line, and filled with second rate, disinterested students who (like myself) were not bright enough to go to university. But it shows a side of the man that is at odds with the current perception of him as a joyless, loveless High Tory with entirely fascist tendencies. In fact, almost unbelievably, he always voted Liberal! He championed the Hippies, for example, every time anyone mentioned them. So be prepared to have many of your ideas about him completely over-turned.

You need some knowledge of the Kabbalah to get the full gist of what follows, and I've included a simple, Gray-inspired summary of this philosophy in the Appendix. But if you skip these parts you will also find chunks of lucid prose that are as good as anything ever written by anyone. Read the following rant about Sex Magic which I had asked him about, as it seemed to be everywhere in those times and I wasn't getting any of it:

I'm afraid I've seen and heard so much bloody rubbish masquerading as Sex Magic, that I'm just about disenchanted with the topic. I think of the great Aleister Crowley sitting up in bed casting I Ching sticks to decide whether he wakes Leah up to poke her or not. I think of skinny old Gerald Gardner, King (?) of the Witches prancing around with elk-horns from a coat-rack tied on his head while the girls tickle his tool with a pink feather duster. I think of all these so-called Master Magicians and High Priests of Witch Covens living on National Assistance and trying to convince themselves they are Adepts and God knows what of Sex Magic when they couldn't even raise a good fart between the lot – let alone anything more dangerously fertile. All because of a pathetic puerility and a lack of genuine love anywhere. Poor, poor little people. God grant them love in their next life-rounds. They need it desperately.

Don't just take in the content, listen to the angry passion, the spontaneous rhythm of his prose. And marvel also at the following advice he gave me, a teenager, at the very beginning of my adventures on what was once termed The Path:

So, be very sure of yourself before seeking entry to the "Inner arenas", and don't say you weren't warned. Once in, there's no turning back. One has to go on, and on, and on, to the bitter bloody end, because one has to. No matter how horrible, how frustrating, or more frequently how blatantly boring the Inner Path may seem, it has to be plodded to the very final and sometimes terrible end before it enters PEACE PROFOUND wherein Nothing can harm or hurt you ever again. You can't just "take up Magic" like some hobby and abandon it when you feel inclined. You may, and periodically should, have "resting" periods during which nothing much appears on the surface while a good deal is developing underneath. Nevertheless, once you become part and parcel of the Magical Tradition, especially that of the West, expect difficulties from all directions. Ultimately you will either overcome or outlive them, even if you re-incarnate a few lives on the way.

He was right there: there was never any turning back in my own life. It hasn't always been happy, but Magic, and the sense of being connected with something bigger than myself, got me through the bad times, gave me numinous adventures and has never been boring. If there is to be a 'bitter bloody end' it will be a small price to pay for the ever-becoming fountains of wonder that the inner traditions have given me.

Yes, some of Bill's jargon-heavy sentences can be hard reading, but his terminologies were all self-created. In fact he was attempting to bring the medieval concepts of that system into the modern age, creating new (if awkward) terms to elucidate insights from his own psyche that were far beyond existing experience. Or *Kabbalah Renovata* as he subtitled his first book. Plus he was attempting to do for Magic what Jung had done for psychotherapy.

And if Jung's writings only made it into the larger world because of the sponsorship of several very rich, adoring females, Gray's managed to get 'out there' by the encouragement of his nemesis Gareth Knight. An irony which was not lost on him. For those who might want more details about their collaboration in several realms, read Knight's compelling autobiography *I Called it Magic*.[3]

This collection of his letters might have been called 'Apprenticed to Magic' if that hadn't been the title of a book by the excellent W.E. Butler. Plus, this would also have implied that Gray was my primary Teacher in this sphere. In fact I owe just as much of a debt to the late and very great Christine Hartley who opened me up in a way that Bill never could.

Yet with these letters I wanted to show the progression of information, insight and wisdom that he passed on without seeking anything in return. Even though I have forgotten many of the things I asked him about, it is still possible to get enormous sense from his replies. The advice he gives is relevant to everyone, even today. Hell, *especially* today! I have retained his idiosyncratic use of capitals, to conjure up the flavour of these missives.

If Bill was a two-fingered typist I have never progressed further than four-fingers with the occasional thumb-flourish. I am still unable to take my eyes from the keyboard. With the advent of word-processing and Optical Character Recognition I was encouraged to attempt the scanning of these letters and save myself a lot of hard work. In the event, their faded condition meant that the scanned material was effectively unreadable. With a big sigh I decided to type each one up by hand, dismayed by the sheer length of some of them, wracked by man-flu, but determined to carry on.

I had ploughed my way through three very lengthy missives, inwardly groaning, when I had a nano-second of Bill's presence behind me. He was pleased, I felt, and smiling. Not from the content but from the effort. Bill always admired effort. I then had the inspiration of changing the settings of the (to me) bewildering

---

3   *I Called it Magic*. Gareth Knight. Skylight Press.

OCR software. That may seem obvious to anyone from a younger, computer literate generation but this was my $E=mc^2$ moment. When I clicked on the appropriate button the options were: *Black & White Document. Color Document.* **Gray Document.** When I chose the latter and jiggled about with the Contrast and Brightness sliders then – lo! – it picked up most of the text beautifully!

Thank you, you Old Sod, I said out loud, relieved. I'm sure I heard a chuckle.

Whatever you think you may know about William G. Gray, put it aside. If I can, for a moment, use the sort of type-style that was second nature to him then be prepared to be VERY SURPRISED by what you are about to LEARN and may you all, one day, find PEACE PROFOUND as a result.

Alan Richardson
Wiltshire
May 2014

Letters of Light

14, Bennington St,
Cheltenham
Glos.

5th Aug 1969

Dear Mr Richardson,

Thank you for your letter of the 30th last. You asked a straight question, so I'll answer it that way.

You will not, to the best of my knowledge and belief find any recommendable magical or other fraternities in this area. Odd groups, "witch covens (!)" and the like perhaps.

If you are genuinely serious, then don't bother with "Groups" and whatnot, but get on by yourself. Genuine Fraternities are established on Inner Dimensions anyway, and your own "lot" will infallibly claim you from inside yourself if you look there.

This will probably sound awfully disappointing to you, but no matter where you go, who you meet, what sort of situations you get into, you will always be thrown back into yourself in the end, so – you might as well start there in the first place and save an awful lot of time, worry, expense, and what have you.

Still – Do what you will – and good luck.

Wm. G. Gray

Everything has to come out of you in any case, because there isn't any other source for it to reach you. Go in and get it, no one will offer it on a plate, and if any claim so to do – suspect them heartily.

Tel; Chelt 24129

14, Bennington St,
Cheltenham
Glos.
GL50 4ED.

Sunday.

Dear Mr Richardson,

Thank you for reply to my last, and for stamp. A stamp is a good idea for getting a letter out of anyone, and certainly to be recommended when dealing with literary folk. Now to deal with your queries.

Yes indeed, the Symbol of an Order or System is the actual means of getting in touch with its real Hierarchy on Inner levels, and far more reliable than chancing an arm among material contacts.[4] I've dealt with this very point in a yet unpublished book, so don't think I pinched the idea from you if and when it comes out. Don't waste time with AMORC (or money on those commercial frauds), the dear old ladies of the TS, or the tweeness of the Maat lot.[5] Go straight to the organ grinder and leave the monkeys to amuse themselves. Use the Tree of Life Glyph of course. What else? It has ALL within it, and is the Key of the West at the moment. Keep the Circle-Cross in mind also. It is the Sign of Cosmos. The Tree-Glyph is there to be <u>used</u> and not merely looked at. Try both. It <u>has</u> to work. I presume you've read my "Ladder of Lights" on it?

I hate to disillusion you, but the real structure of the Occult Orders is not on physical levels for obvious reasons. You have to go INSIDE Life to meet them truly. Human beings of such calibre don't incarnate any more than they can help. They are of much greater value where and as they are.

Don't bother with the "Inner Light" lot either. They are very far indeed from anything that D.F. stands for. Few genuine initiates stay with them very long. True they serve a purpose, but surely you can

---

4   I figured that by mentally projecting the symbol of a Magical Order into the aethers, I would be able to make contact with the Inner Chiefs behind it.

5   The House of Maat, London based, details of which I have long since forgotten.

do better than that dismal and depressing crew of self-righteous and semi sanctimonious souls. They are at least honest about money, as they can afford to be while supported by chiefly one very wealthy patron, but of all the gloomy and suppressive gatherings I ever attended, the present Inner Light set up takes some beating! Dion Fortune dead has more vitality and energy than all the I.L. lot have while still in this world. For heaven's sake look higher than that for LIGHT.

You more than probably do have the techniques in yourself. Dig them out and start using them. Better to fall over your own feet than have someone else put the boot in.

St Paul's? Hm, Yes. I live a few hundred yards from it. Can't honestly say I'm vastly impressed by such of its students as I have unavoidably met. But then, I suppose places are much of a muchness these days. Why are students so damn dreary and dopey? Why are they not alive? You probably know more of this than I do, being closer to the issue.

If you should go to St Paul's, you will be welcome to visit me if you like, but I warn you that you will do so at your own risk. Few come back for more, and those few are valued. The Law of Life is not "DO AS THOU WILT" for what might be imagined, but: "BE WHAT THOU WILT WITHIN THEE." That makes all the difference.

It all depends what you WILL TO BE. I've metaphorically booted more would-be occultists out of my doors than I can remember. Witches, bitches, twitches, and all their odd little itches I couldn't care less about. (Though I've met most of the self-styled "Witches", and actually kept on more or less friendly terms with rare examples.) The INTENT or WILL is what matters. With RIGHT INTENT the Way of Light can be followed. May you find PEACE PROFOUND therein.

Sincerely,

Wm. G. Gray

14, Bennington St,
Cheltenham
Glos.
GL50 4ED.

Sept 28

Dear Alan Richardson

Thanks for yours of 22nd, read yesterday when I returned from holiday at Brighton. Also for S.A.E. Will try and tackle your queries sequentially, insofar as anyone can deal with the Inner problems of another which are uniquely their own, even if paralleled by millions of other souls.

Your contact system is quite reasonable for a beginning effort, certainly better than mine were once.[6] Perhaps improvable by a sort of staging process in approach. After all, the so-called "Four Worlds" are only arbitrary markings at points of "Arising to Light", and not really separate from each other at all. They are only references connecting Humanity to Divinity, and you might think of them as markings on a meter reading from Zero to Infinity. Suppose you try mentally equating them with states of "solidity", such as:

EXPRESSION	(Assiah)	Normal solidity of matter.	Human.
FORMATION	(Yetzirah)	Liquidity.	Angelic.
CREATION	(Briah)	Gaseity.	Archangelic.
ORIGINATION	(Atziluth)	Radiation.	Divine.

For instance, take the physical Symbol (the Sun), imagine yourself sunbathing on a pleasant beach, (as I was last week). Out of the sea (liquid – WATER) comes an angel bearing a measure of some kind (one of the Malakim). This being leads you into the sunlit sea and you flow out into it, "at-one-ing". Then comes Michael with burning breastplate with solar symbol on it, and smiles at you with his strongly kind blue eyes, (he has golden hair,) and with his fiery power draws you out of the sea into the vapour of the AIR by his spear-staff. From

---

6   I had sent him a simple path-working which involved stepping through a hexagram.

16

that point on, he leads you through the Hexagram, up the six steps, or what you will, into the Presence of the Divine One of this point.

The OMNISCIENT. (Eloah va Daath.) You do <u>NOT</u> attempt to look at this Presence, only feel Its radiance. Michael stands behind you with a kindly hand over your eyes. Eventually, he turns you round and starts you back to your beach, where you wake up the better for the experience. Try this anyway. You can easily alter the bits and pieces to suit yourself, but follow the principles behind it.

By the way, don't attempt to "hear words", just "get it by contact". The contact will sort itself out into English via your mind in its own time. In fact it is silly to expect English or any other human language on that level, for no one speaks like that there. Once you build up your symbolic translating machine via the "Letters", and so forth, the sense will "come English" all right.

Your second problem is more serious. I thought you were all set to becoming a teacher via St Paul's here???? Has that one gone for a Burton?[7]

The only answer to all the nuts and weirdies "attracted to the occult" is SO WHAT? Who the Hell cares about them except them, and sometimes I doubt that. Do you <u>have</u> to associate yourself with them apart from the general categories of humanity? Just <u>DON'T</u> be drawn into anything they do with their own piffling little activities. Why bother with it? Get back and take a long look at them – then let them dig their graves their own way. They have the right to ruin themselves if they Will, and you are under no obligation whatever to do one thing about it unless they appeal for help – which they probably won't, because they enjoy their muddling.

DON'T be bulldozed around by ridiculous insinuations that Occultism causes insanity and so forth. It doesn't and never did. It will, however, provide ample means for unstable people to go right over the top altogether. Conversely, it affords the same people every possible means of building themselves up into very stable, balanced, and perfecting people indeed. Everything depends on what the intention is, and the Will of the individual.

---

7   When I was unable to go to King Alfred's College, Winchester, for personal reasons, I thought about St Paul's to be near Gray and thus learn magic. When I found that St Paul's was all male I promptly applied to the Northern Counties College in Newcastle, where the ratio of females to males was 4-1.

A main point is to keep your trap <u>firmly shut</u> about your occult interests, except to those you can absolutely trust with your own life – and how many of those do you know? Discuss anything <u>but</u> the Occult with others unless they are very close to you indeed. Do you know, in a monastery, the one topic of conversation monks <u>don't</u> discuss is religion? A good rule. They say that religion is something to <u>live</u>, not argue about. The same might be said for the Occult. It all depends on what you want it for, and this vital motive only <u>you</u> can know.

You want to practice the Occult? Very well, do so on your own responsibility, and by your own efforts, but don't be impressed or over-influenced by all the beards and weird in the Hippy, Zippy, or even the Dippy scene. They have their own dree to weird. (Ugh!) Incidentally – lay off pot or whatever peppery pills might be proffered. They only make for Mickey Mouse stuff in the Otherworld, apart from wrecking the psyche beyond belief. Oddly enough, I was asking myself only the other day, did one single really worthwhile achievement ever come out of a drugged mind? One wonderful poem? One remarkable scientific discovery? One great piece of literature? Sculpture? Painting? Engineering? Astronautics? Anything? ---- I'm still waiting to discover anything whatever of the slightest good or use reaching us via the Paths of Confusion. Maybe you can think of something, but I can't. It just isn't worth the waste of a whole lifetime.

Remember I've seen most of this scene, and am just not impressed by any of it. There are worthwhile jobs to do in the Occult, and there are worthwhile people trying to do them. I just try and do the job immediately set before me, and let the rest get on with itself. It will, if you WILL.

Don't worry too much. You've got a far better grasp than most. Best wishes

Wm. G. Gray

By the way, where did you get my address from?[8]

---

8   A second-hand copy of the magazine *New Dimensions*. It contained a small ad saying that the writer William G. Gray would answer any poignant queries. So I sent him a poignant query.

14, Bennington St,
Cheltenham
Glos.
GL50 4ED.

Feb 24th 70

Your Query:
Archangelic attribution to the Sephirah TIPHERETH[9]

Dear Alan Richardson.

We'll do better than answer your query directly. Tell you how to find
the answer for yourself, which is always the best way for everyone.

1. Start from a known, believed, or undoubted basis, such as:

TIPHERETH is the Solar Sphere.

2. Find an Archangel with a maximum of Solar characteristics and:

3. Ask this Being where its affinities are. There will be your answer.

I would suggest you visit your nearest reference Library, or beg and
borrow access to all the books giving information about Archangels
and their characteristics you can.

Note down all the salient points you can discover about MICHAEL
and RAPHAEL. There is a surprising amount available to anyone
taking this trouble. Get pictures of them, artists' impressions, folktales.
Check the Mishnah, Torah, Book of Angels and the Encyclopaedia
Britannica. Don't forget Legends for children. All and any available
sources. This will provide you with a mass of information which you
will have to classify, codify, and generally mess around with until very

---

9   I was bewildered by some authorities placing Raphael there, and others
     Michael.

definite impressions and opinions fire up in your own mind about those two Archangels.

Eventually you will feel them building up in your mind, and the mental images you form will be the Telesmic Images through which the Entities of Inner Existence they represent (which are the real "Archangels") may make contact with your consciousness. When you feel able to shut your eyes and "call up" or "evoke" a clear image of Michael in your mind – do so, and demand of it which particular Sephiroth it associates with – and why. See what comes through. It will only answer you from the information you have "banked" with yourself, but the way that information comes out and the new knowledge you gain from this should have come from the "Michael-Concept" in our Cosmic, (or as Jung would have said: "Collective") Consciousness.

When you have done all this, and got an answer that satisfies you, together with a sound reason for it, let me know and we will compare notes. Remember the answer required is the correct Archangelic Concept for the Solar Sephirah TIPHERETH. (Harmonious Beauty.)

Why the difference of opinion? Because in the case of Dion Fortune, when she wrote the Mystical Qabalah, DF was an enthusiastic "esoteric Christian" believing in "spiritual healing" and taking Raphael to be the Patron of healing, and consequently the central or Solar Figure in her conception of Cosmos. Therefore she associated Raphael with the Sun – which is more than others did. In her enthusiasm for Christo-conception and centring everything on the Christ Image, (remember that Christ was a Divine-Healer Image), Dion Fortune either skimped research or chose to overlook one important point. Raphael is a healer of hurts, not diseases. Michael heals diseases. So – Raphael became her centre-figure, and her Society of the Inner Light took over this when they continued with her book (of which they had copyright and therefore benefit by sales) as their principle text for Qabalistic teaching.

W. Butler was a personal disciple of Dion Fortune's, and also ex Inner Light. I think you will find that only Inner Lighters use Raphael at Tiphereth. Should be interested to find Raphael attributes elsewhere. Michael has always been the Solar Figure in every other Group-working.

I enclose a leaflet of Archangelic interest and recent printing. The prints do not do justice to the really amazing originals. These are actually going to be gradually altered on account of many weaknesses in the designs you see. The artist is a really remarkable man in himself, but is not a Qabalist, and did the paintings for a special commission. There is one really glaring error from the symbolic angle. See if you can spot it! The mistake was not deliberate, but merely from lack of adequate information. No more. Yet that is how so many errors get into occult books. Lack of original research and personal practice, for which there is no substitute whatsoever.

Good luck

Wm. G. Gray

P.S. you forgot to put your address on your letter or S.A.E. Have found an old note of yours and hope it is the same. Lucky, I usually throw out all mail after I've answered – often before![10]

---

10 I left the SAE blank so he would type my name and address and make it look blandly official. My mother was so terrified of the strange mail I was getting from myriad sources that I would watch for the postie coming, sneak down and pull the letter silently through the box. I had broken the spring so it wouldn't make a noise. If I was caught, I could pretend it was literature to do with the RAF (another passion of mine) and had fake documents that I could swap over with prestidigitatory skills.

14, Bennington St,
Cheltenham
Glos.

[Undated]

Dear Alan Richardson.

(Thank you for S.A.E.)

Very good work on your part! It is really encouraging to see at least someone coming along reasonably prepared to take up the Work those of "my lot" will have to leave behind us in this world during the next few years. It makes us feel we haven't entirely wasted our lives and efforts, frequently as we may have wondered about that point. I hope you do much better than we did (remember our youth was busted apart by two World Wars!)

Yes, Michael is shown with a Sword instead of a Spear-Staff (Rod). Frank Regardie[11] ought to have spotted that, but he seemed to have missed it. Have you read any of his classics? He really is the most lovable and laughable chap you could wish to meet. Has kept his slight Cockney accent after all these years abroad. (He practices in Frisco.)

I didn't mean to warn you off the Inner Light at all. My own experience of them is only the way they rubbed off on me. Trouble is, I can't stand "twee" conglomerations of old ladies and what I call "drippy" wishy-washy holier-than-thous. Maybe they've altered by now, though I doubt it. I knew a Scot who joined, and he was about the dourest, grimmest, most silent, and unsmiling piece of rigid-principled "Wee Free" you could imagine. Sin and he were total strangers. I thought at least he would rise to Magus if not Ipsissimus of the I.L. in double-quick time, but to my amazement, he resigned after somewhat less than a year. Two things I grant the I.L.: Strict honesty about money, and an entirely unsentimental approach to almost everything. Their principles are unassailable from the most critical Victorian moralist, but alas – most mortals need something <u>rather</u> more humanly warm-hearted.

---

11 Israel Regardie, known to his intimates as Francis, or just Frank.

Yes, why didn't you try and make your Figures stand on their heads? Have a go at this, and when they refuse to obey silly or undignified suggestions, you'll know their "Inners" are taking up the Images you obligingly made for them to occupy.

Actually the Caduceus for Raphael is accurate enough. Raphael is Hermes under another guise. (How Hermes loves disguising himself! He is personally my favourite God despite his fondness for tricky and cunning activities.)

I might warn you my enumeration of the Paths is NOT the same as the published G.D. stuff. It is geared to the English Letter System, and Tarot as per my Rit.Mag.Meth.[12] The Paths are indeed important. Very. I'm nearly finishing the companion to the "Ladder" which deals entirely with the Paths. Hard work.

Best Wishes

Wm. G. Gray

---

12 His brilliant and unsurpassed *Magical Ritual Methods.*

14, Bennington St,
Cheltenham
Glos.

[Undated]

Dear Alan

Thank you for your letter and SAE. Attributions of anything to anything else are only worth your own fundamental and implicit belief therein. If others have similar beliefs, then a number of individuals can share in the same attributions. It is like speaking languages. If a lot of people agree on meanings attributable to common sonic symbols – it works. Otherwise not. The whole question with "occult" symbols is this. They have to be shared by human souls and "intelligences" existing in quite different states of being. In other words, if you (or anyone) metaphorically hold up one end of a symbol, just <u>who</u> in conditions of "otherlife" is going to connect with the other? Unless such a contact occurs, you will be in touch with no one but yourself. Will the "other holder" in fact be a type you would want to link up with?? You get the point?

To ensure (as far as anything can be possibly ensured in these matters) that all contacts made are reasonably reliable and beneficial, the Tree-System has been linked with "Keywords" associated with the finest and best ideas or principles inherent in humanity reaching for Divinity. A workable relationship has been established between them all via the Points (Spheres) and Paths, and the rest left to individuals for establishing their own communications of consciousness. That's it.

If, say, you personally really associated Michael (or anything else) with Netzach because of <u>your own deep beliefs, experience, and conscious convictions</u> on that issue then the association would work for you, if no one else except those who believed in you, and their belief would be limited by yourself.

If, on the other hand you attached Michael to Netzach on external levels of awareness, while at the same time "unconsciously" denying this deep down inside of you, then you would only harm your own psyche. A lot of our troubles come from affirming something outwardly while entirely denying it with our deep Inner consciousness in far closer contact to truth.

First of all of course, one has to take a certain amount of what others say as information, for the simple reason that's all we have to begin with. Out of that lot, must come the really vital issues of personal experience which make us what we are. Faith translated into Inner actualities. At the same time, awakening Inner intelligence should help us be selective and discriminative as to what to accept and reject.

For me, and others, the Raphael-Hod-Air etc chain of consciousness works perfectly. It makes sense and replies with reason. It is demonstrable.

In old times, it was once a custom to deliberately make a wrong attribution or so in any System in order to exclude those who would be unwelcome within it. Those who were naturally acceptable within the System would soon spot this and alter it accordingly, and those who hadn't the wits or wisdom to do this automatically excluded themselves until they either learned otherwise or packed it in altogether.

Remember that Qabalah is NOT a mass-production "come one come all" affair, but a spiritual selection system for souls to sort themselves into their correct Cosmic categories. Thus, the fact that some have been relatively content to accept Hod-Water or anything else should tell you (as it tells the "Inners") just what sort of enquiring entities they amount to. Don't attempt to correct them any more than you would whisper an examination answer into a candidate's ear. It's their reactive test, let them get on with it. Believe in yourself and what you have learned there, and more will come along to alter and improve what you already have. Give it time.

From what I know of the "Order of the Cubic Stone" (!) they haven't a thing to teach you, and don't be impressed by any of their silly claims. Their "Warden"[13] doesn't even know what "Goetia" means, and is barely capable of English let alone anything else. It was an excruciating experience hearing him screeching what he believed were "Enochian Keys". Nor did he know what "Enoch" meant. Sorry, but I don't rate them very highly.

---

13 David Edwards – whose little books I rather liked.

So many of groups today are mainly remnants of other Groups "having a go" on their own. There isn't one I'd trust among the whole boiling of them on past experience of their behaviour. They, on the other hand, can't stand me because of my insistence on ethical codes and capabilities they are unwilling to support, and my uncompromising attitudes to muddled motivations and insincerity or unreliability of character. Nor have I time for "wishy-washyness" and dilettante ditherings. This makes me so damned rude on occasions that recipients have good reason to remember the event. Best compliment in years came back to me – "He's an absolute old bastard – but one has to admit he might know something."

I'm very unlikely to read anything you write in *Quest* or its disgusting competitor *Insight*.[14] Remember I've met all these people at first hand and so formed opinions on a very personal basis. None of them are bad or wicked folk or in any sense wrong or evil. I simply found them irritating, puerile, incompetent and hopelessly inaccurate in all I was able to observe of their activities. This is simply my own opinion. You are in no way bound to agree with it and have to find things out from your angle. It might also help you understand if you ever mention my name anywhere and receive a disgusted "Oh him!" in reply.

In case you're wondering by this time if I know anybody I respect or approve of in the "Occult World" the answer is yes I do, but they have nothing to do with any form of publicity or chicanery, and the last thing they would belong to are little "Groups" or phoney "Orders". That sort of thing is strictly for the "pseuds". Correspondence courses, secret initiations, join now pay later, instant mediumship etc etc – all this is the garbage heap of "occultism". Finding a bargain there is like looking for one in the Portobello Road markets on Saturday. It can be done, providing the stall-holder doesn't know what they are offering.

My advice, based on a hard lifetime, is meet who you like, join what you like, providing you realise they can't offer you a thing you couldn't have got out of yourself with less effort. All the "Occult knowledge" in existence is obtainable IN YOU. Don't expect revelations from anyone else. Don't think they've got something you

---

14 I thoroughly enjoyed both and wrote for both.

haven't and can't obtain by your own efforts. Don't rely on books for teaching except insofar as these may help you get it from your own Inner sources. Old Abra Melin was fundamentally right in his HGA principles.[15]

Already you are better informed and have more working ideas along these lines than many much older people I have met flaunting all kinds of claims. Keep going, and let me know how you make out. Hope I've helped somewhat. What happened about your examinations, and what career are you settling into?

14, Bennington St,
Cheltenham
Glos.

25 May 70

Dear Alan Richardson,

Thank you for your letter of 22nd, and SAE. It is usually possible to find some time for answering genuine enquiries such as yours, but I have a feeling that most occult writers no longer reply to most of the rubbish received. The genuine matter like yours is regrettably rare, while the junk is sometimes overwhelming. Just the same thing happens in Otherworld contacts. For every really deep and relevant one received, there is a whole mass of muddled meaninglessness. Hence the necessity for the Qabalistic System, which aims at keeping contact solely with worthwhile Inner contacts and filtering out the remainder. Like the selective tuning of a radio where the balance between inductive and capacitive factors determine the frequency of working. If you think of the Spheres as principles of Capacity, and the Paths as principles of Inductance, there is a nice analogy to use for "tuning in".

No, the H.G.A. is not a simple Inner contact such as you describe, but a specific Inner entity in its own right. Not a "spirit Guide" such as the dear old ladies love to have, and whose platitudes would bore me blue and unnatural piety irritate me. The H.G.A. is normally your Inner "Sponsor" from an order of being on rather different Life-levels than human. It is not an ex-human soul transmogrified so to speak into an Angel, but an entitised Intelligence outside incarnationary living, yet concerned with selection of spiritually evolving human souls for continuance of Cosmos. Old Abraham the Jew gave about the best account of the H.G.A. possible in his Abramelin System, which no doubt you have read. In one sense, "Conversation and Knowledge" etc is an activity of one's own Higher Self, because only this very advanced part of ourselves can make serious contact with such Innerlife entities.

It is scarcely fair to take my own case for comparative purposes, because the linkage is probably genetic, running through my mother's line. She had what her ancestors termed "the Sight", a gift I refuse to inherit any more than I can help, because at human level it reveals too many horrible possibilities ahead. I had enough of it in the last War. As a rule, "interest in the Occult" is "in the family" one way or another. Even today there are families in which traces of very old pagan faiths have been handed down from generation to generation despite all the surface Christianity. Sometimes you may hear of such folk being called "Witch" families, but they are NOT, and NEVER WERE "Witches" in the sense of evil-doers and baddies. They simply believed in what to them was the "Old Wisdom", or the faith of their remoter ancestors. No, mine is not one of those families as such. I suppose I must have been about 15 also from individual dedication point, which was simply a "pick-up" from where I left off last time around.

Good wishes

Wm. G. Gray

14, Bennington St,
Cheltenham
Glos.

Date as postmark

Dear Alan,

(Most people do call me "Bill".) You do ask $64,000 queries!!!

The Holy Guardian Angel amounts to what we would call nowadays your own personification of your own Inner relationships with higher states of spiritual consciousness reaching you from other sources of Entity/ies directing you toward Divinity as an Individuant of Life.

This sounds complicated. In fact it is a Telesmic Image created between your consciousness, and (in effect) that of Divinity attracting your attention towards Itself. A sort of spiritual "Symbol", real enough so far as existence of Energy is real, which acts as a mediative means between your "ordinary" Self-status, and your own highest possible Identity. Put in childish terms (which are often clearest) the HGA is something (or someone) you and God invent between you as a communicating agency. An "artificial" creation if you like, but none the less important for that. A kind of mutual conception of each other between Microcosm and Macrocosm.

There is great psychological truth in the "Abramelin" system, if understood properly. Nevertheless, its provisos still hold true in this century. Do not attempt to follow it literally unless you really are in a position to isolate yourself independently as the thesis outlines. You can forget the "Magic Squares" "come-on". The whole system is designed to make people recognise the spiritual truths inside themselves, if they have enough determination and devotion. It deals with "spiritual alchemy" or transmuting the worst in ourselves into the best we can become.

Actually, the Abramelin system is designed for exactly the type of person specified – someone of sufficient means and intelligence to carry it out. Otherwise it does not apply to people except in general principles. The "Demons" controlled and commanded are in fact your own worst possible propensities. The rite is an exercise in calling these into objectivity and neutralising their effects before putting them into opposite courses. In effect, it means that if we could live beneficially with all the energy we put to destructive and wrong uses, we should become the perfect people we were supposed to be in the first place. That is the "Secret Magic" of the Abramelin system, disguised with a lot of double-talk.

At this time of your life, you would be wisest to get your diploma first, and keep your occult interests very much to yourself, especially from the "establishment" and its representatives. The first thing you would have to learn in any reputable association of "initiates" is what used to be called "sacred secrecy", or keeping counsel. It means that in effect you live Life on many levels, each having its own significance and values. You keep energies of each confined to that particular circle, reflecting into others only through their terms. For instance, you would not on any account speak of "Magic" topics as such to those outside your own "Magic" circle. If you had to communicate "occult" information with "outsiders", you would only do so in their terms of reference, never in "initiated" fashion.

For instance, I would never evince the least interest in occult or Magical issues other than with those concerned. I might admit vaguely an interest in "metaphysics" or something seeming too dull and abstruse to be worth talking about. By and large, I do not speak of the occult at all. Among those who already know, there is no need to speak, and among those who do not know, there is a need not to speak. Now there is a nice dilemma for you, or a paradox, whatever.

Have you ever thought what the major motivation behind Man's interest in Magic is??? Brutally and basically it is an attempt to compensate his own inadequacies from superior sources of supply. Well, why not? What is really wrong with a sick man wanting to be well, a stupid man wanting wisdom, or a miserable man wanting happiness and peace? Nothing. The trouble comes when a vicious man wants opportunities of evil, a brutal man seeks victims, an unhappy man wants to make others suffer, and so forth. That one degree of deflection at initiating intention level, makes all the difference between "White" and "Black" Magic.

About the first Question any genuine Initiate asks of someone claiming "an interest in Magic" or suchlike, is: "Why? What is the reason you want to join Groups and work Magic? What do you suppose you can do with it?" As a rule, one gets some sort of: "Because I want to help others, and do good," or crap of the like kind. They think that is what they ought to say or what the hearer wants to hear, or thereabouts. Deep down, they know the reason well enough, but only when they confront themselves with their own Inner reality are they likely to get anywhere worthwhile.

Have you ever noted how the feeblest, most futile, and pathetic creatures of both sexes all want to "go in for healing" and gather in tragic little corners waving useless hands and faded imaginations over the heads of hopeless humans? It is so sad that a stone would cry if it could.

That's about all I can manage at present. I've just completed contract about a third book this year, "The Rollright Ritual". Something quite different about Stone Circle working. It's a shared finance affair, which won't produce profit for about three years, but will then pay well. Or should. Still waiting for details on other two which ought to be out about the end of year or beginning of next.

Good wishes

Bill Gray

14, Bennington St,
Cheltenham
Glos.

Aug 16th 70

Dear Alan Richardson,

Thank you for your last letter. As you see, I am enclosing a copy of my "Office of the Holy Tree of Life" which Sangreal published well enough except for the poor style of binding. So far as is known, it is the first liturgical work of Qabalah ever printed, and I hope it will be helpful. Do note however, that the Paths are geared to the English, and not the Hebrew Alphabet. The reason for this is simply that we are, after all, an English-speaking and thinking people, and if conscious communication along those lines is needed with Inner Intelligences, then appropriate symbology must be used. Anyway, I hope it will help you.

I see your problem, I think. You are, and will continue to be, whatever "Grade" your own experience of both Inner and outer Light-Life make you. No ceremonial psycho-drama will ever make you an "Initiate" of anything. You make yourself an Initiate as you go along. Ceremonial occasions termed "Initiations" are traditionally formal affairs of Group-consciousness for linking souls with specific lines of "Light-Life" between External and Internal Entity. No more. Nothing, in fact, that any soul of reasonable ability could not do for itself if it so willed. Traditional "Initiation" is more or less a Group way of saying: "We like you and believe you are capable of living along our special lines. Come with us if you Will." That is all. There is only one real Initiator: Life itself. Take the Tree-System for instance:

You are a living entity in this particular Earth-world. That is the Initiation of Malkuth the Kingdom.

You are a human being, with specific ancestral and other chains of Life before and behind you and within you. That is the Initiation of Yesod the Foundation or Establishment of life on which you are based.

You are an <u>intelligent being</u>, or you could not survive in this world for long. That is the Initiation of Hod, and the Glory of living.

You are a <u>feeling</u> being, or you would never develop as a soul, capable of living in ever evolving conditions of Cosmos. That is the Initiation of Netzach, or the Victory and Achievement which makes living really worthwhile.

As you will realise by now, every average human has got some degree of those first four Initiations. Now comes the crunch. Who is able to formulate those four into Cosmic orbit so to speak around a central nucleus of "Spiritual Solar Energy" or Living Power-Purpose represented by Tiphereth, the Initiation of Balanced Beauty, or Holy Harmony? How many humans are really able to centre their lives about a pivotal purpose of radiant Inner Reality illuminating Mankind with the Meaning of our existence???

This is the Initiation of Tiphereth, the Beauty behind our being alive at all. Many have this to some degree, but how many can you think of without it, or even an intention of looking for it???? You see?

It all interlocks. The better you are able to gain finer degrees of Malkuth-Yesod-Hod-Netzach experience of Life-Initiation, the more you will have to cosmate yourself around the Tiphereth Cosmic Centre with. Thus, you can't very well "go back" if you are continuing to evolve in those first four Spheres up the Tree. You might as well say it would be regression to re-study or gain fresh experience with any subject in which you have now reached A-level (congratulations!) Once you find your central Life-purpose with a recognisable Divine Intention behind it, then you will automatically begin initiating yourself into the Tiphereth Sphere.

And so on and so on. You must have some (even the smallest conceivable) degree of initiation into all the Spheres. It is simply a question of extending these along your Life-Light-Line.

Best wishes for your forthcoming teacher's training. The experience in a mental hospital should be invaluable to you, providing it doesn't lead you into the trap of compulsively tying mental labels round everyone's neck and thinking this entitles you or anyone to take others for granted. Too many psychiatrists are too fond of this. Obviously those with unsuitable mental equipment for coping with our so-called civilisation (and God knows this takes some doing) should be entitled to asylum among other humans who created those conditions, but this does not mean they should be penalised for their inadequacies. Certainly dangerous or criminally insane creatures have to be treated with responsible precautions, and it is necessary to know how to make definitions of category within accurate limits, but we must never exclude the "Element of Inner Evolution", which makes all the difference between the "Yes" and "No" of assessment.[16]

We may fairly say for example: "Here is someone my judgement and experience tells me is a so-and-so. Now then, do they, or do they not have the capability or Will to evolve beyond that point toward any finer state of being???" Everything depends on this vital Inner possibility, and how many humans are able to answer the question with absolute certainty? While we grow we Live. Inwardly or Outwardly, physically, mentally, and spiritually. If and when we refuse or reject, or dissociate ourselves from this Life-process, then we begin to die from within, as a tree does, and our ultimate elimination from the Plan of Existence comes so much closer. No need to worry about this though. Soul-suicide is no easy affair, and it can't be done without intention any more than physical suicide is possible inadvertently.

I hope I've been some help anyway. Don't talk of "repaying me" for anything. Just do the same and better for someone else when your turn comes along in due course, which it most certainly will in very positive ways.

Good luck.

---

16 At several times in my life I have worked as a Nursing Auxiliary (as they called it then) in various Mental Hospitals – as they were then termed. Far more interesting and less stressful than teaching! I have worked with extremely violent patients, full-blown psychopaths and many murderers, but none of them caused me the grief that class 4Q (no pun!) of Saintbridge School, Gloucester inflicted.

14, Bennington St,
Cheltenham
Glos.

29 9 70

Dear Alan Richardson,

Thank you for letter and SAE.

NO. There is nothing like the real G.D.[17] in physical existence now, for many reasons.

BUT, there will be published in the New Year a very complete and conscientious account of existent "Orders", Groups, Societies, and what-not in England. Obtainable from Watkins of London when it comes out. Neither the author, nor I for that matter, are impressed by any of them, but the book is quite sincere, and so is the author, who is known to me personally. It might help you choose which brand of rubbish to go for. Both author and I are agreed that it may be best for youngsters to do things the hard way, join various Groups, waste time and money, learn more sense, go through disillusionment, then come out on their own and start doing things properly, having got their mistakes out of their systems. Best of luck to you.

Magical memory.[18] The only true way to "catch up" with it is "grow into it". It is utterly unhelpful otherwise. The older you grow, the more it "comes back". Last life memories are very little use to anyone I've found. If you look forward long enough, the circle of consciousness catches up with you through your past. Keep facing the Right-Light Path.

If your writing is bad (like mine) invest in a typewriter. This one is 50 years old and will see my life out yet.[19]

Best wishes

Wm. G. Gray

---

17 Hermetic Order of the Golden Dawn
18 I had asked him about past lives, and how to remember them.
19 It did. He was very proud of his old Remington.

14, Bennington St,
Cheltenham
Glos. GL50 4ED

12th. Nov. 1970

Dear Alan Richardson,

What is a Kingdom without a Crown, or a Crown with no Kingdom to rule? Not a Zen Chouan [sic], but a Qabalistic Query (which amounts to much the same).[20]

Kether and Malkuth are theoretically changeable or transmutable when their completion-circuit of Cosmos is closed by mutual contact. The whole of one Existence is but a single unit of another one Otherwise. If the whole of a "Malkuth" is a human Earthlife (say) this is only an infinite fraction of the "Kether" to be attained by uncountable incarnations. All those Malkuths in Kether "after another fashion" as the text says. On the other hand we make "micro-attainments" maybe each day of a life. Lots of little "Kethers", going toward the make-up of a "Malkuth" life. Malkuth and Kether are first and last PRINCIPLES, which may be applied through all extensions of Existence in whatsoever proportions are necessary to preserve the Pattern of the Plan. To "Zero-out" into the Ainsophaur [sic] is another process. Think of the Ainsophaur as the "PERFECT PEACE PROFOUND", Nirvana, or what you will. As we come to the top of any Life-scale, "Kether", we only find ourselves at the bottom of another one, "Malkuth", ad infinitum until the Ultimation of Zero is achieved.[21]

---

20 As best as I can recall, I was asking him about the concept of the Malkuth in our universe being the Kether of another – and conversely so. While I could understand not being able to grasp 'our' ultimate realm of Kether, I wondered how I could be aware of that universe 'below' us which saw *our* realm as the ultimate. No, I don't worry about it now.

21 I would guess from the tortuous prose he was working on his *Tree of Evil* at the time which, although a work of genius, needs real determination to penetrate the style. Then again, he was bringing into our awareness concepts that no-one else had even thought of, so he was always going to be damned for the new language which he struggled so determinedly to create.

Let's not worry about that for a while, shall we? Take it for granted and get on with the difficult job of human living in these confusing conditions of Creation.

The "Overself" was coined as a "Blanket-term" to mean the One Self, or Single Life Spirit, out of which every entitised entity (that's us!) emanated. Granted all these terms are confusing. Personally I think the good old "Body, Mind, Soul and Spirit" take some beating for simplicity, and I'm all for simplification where this is practical. Also the use of Western terms for preference.

Yes I had your other letter. Thank you. My "Seasonal Occult Rituals" are now out about a fortnight ago. By the way, I doubt if Frank Regardie has taken part in any occult Rites for many years. Dion Fortune was the principal agent in this country who tried to get Magic on a workable and practical basis as a sound mystical modus vivendi rather than weekend occult theatricals. Crowley was mainly trying to reconcile his ideas of God with the "Satan-sin" he was made to believe sex was when a child. It will probably be difficult for you, a modern, to realise just how much terror and distortion could be "brain-washed" into sensitive children on the subject of sex by "religious" people, particularly Plymouth Brethren or narrow nonconformist folk, in the days when Crowley was young. Hence his life-long battle of beliefs.

Lobsang Rampa – or Cyril Hoskins if I remember the name rightly. Providing you realise his works are ones of very pleasant creative imagination – fair enough. An Inner world he found most helpful when he was very ill a long while back. He went to Ireland later I believe, but don't know if he is still incarnate or not. Never met him personally. Of course he claimed that his "Hoskins" personality died altogether, and "Rampa" stepped smartly into the body and took it over. This I doubt extremely, but do not doubt that an extension of consciousness did link him with Inner areas of awareness that he found most fascinating, and an account of which he wrote up in rather delightful ways.[22]

Hope you find "Magical Ritual Methods" helpful. Perhaps in the years to come you will write yourself about all the improvements and developments which you have added to it. At least it is a start,

---

22 I've still got Rampa's letters too. I won't have a word said against him!

and somebody will have to go on with the work <u>somewhere</u>. It took years to accumulate all that information and experience which can be read in a very short time. So much Malkuth for so little Kether. Think today, how long did it take to acquire all the information to program a computer which gives you a working result in seconds? How many people for how long had to think all those thoughts one at a time so that now — all you want is there at asking? Suppose this were reversible, and Someone thought just <u>One</u> thought which took multimillions of minds millions of millennia to catch up with and equate???? Well? Do you get the connection?

At the moment I am in between chapters of next book, and can only go as fast as it "comes through". Therefore I cannot promise much time for dealing with queries. There is a lot to be done. Keep going though. Your share will most certainly be given you of the work later. Of that you need have no doubt at all, but don't expect anything dramatic. It's far more likely to "sneak up" on you quite quietly.

Best wishes.

Wm G. Gray

14, Bennington St,
Cheltenham
Glos.

[Undated…possibly March 1971]

Dear A.R.

Thanks for your enquiries and SAE. Something a little odd occurred to me at once. About a year or so ago, you would have been able to answer two of your queries for yourself. The Michael-Tiphereth one, and the Central Sun idea. Also, you would have been able to put them in a clear and unambiguous fashion. What you have to answer <u>for yourself</u> now, is exactly <u>why</u> areas of uncertainty should have arisen in you, and just <u>what</u> would prompt you to ask for clearance on points no one can clear for you except yourself. Why have you "complicated up" a clear enough issue otherwise?[23]

One is a straightforward decision. Can you, or can you not work with a different set of fundamental concepts to those you find acceptable for your own use. This is a Yes-No issue simply. Which only you can decide. Why can't or don't you?

Supposing you approach the XYZ Order of the Golden Whatsit and say: "You ask me to work this way, but I'm already working that one. Can we compromise?" They, in the conventional style tell you they couldn't possibly have anything to do with you unless you are prepared to start at Square 1 as they specify. What then? Ask yourself simply <u>can</u> you scrap all you already have? And so what were your beliefs worth in the first place? You may, on the other hand, find some good reason for yourself why you <u>should</u> alter your ideas to angles you prefer. If so, there's no problem.

Your second query: "What is the Central Sun" is about as unanswerable as a Zen koan <u>as you have phrased it</u>. Where else is any Sun but centrally in the Cosmos? Have you not a Solar centre in your

---

23 Quite simply I had been two-timed and dumped by Lorraine B. The queries were just an excuse for a broken-hearted teen to make contact with an understanding soul. Plus I hoped his formidable clairvoyance might give me some comfort. It didn't.

Self? How else does your own energy emerge from your Nil-nucleus? How does Nuclear Energy "Become" itself anyway?

Points for guidance. You are being "trained" for a teacher. "Training" implies indoctrination for specific purposes. What authority is "training" you to teach what and to whom??? Why? Why are millions of public money put to this use? Remember that teachers are automatically agents of authorities paying their salaries, and these authorities expect return for their outlay of expense in terms of conditioned consciousness to suit ends they are scarcely prepared to either reveal or discuss. You personally may be idealistic and altruistic, motivated by the noblest intentions, but your employers have very different objectives. Their aim is necessarily the establishment of a socialised citizenry entirely amenable to whatever patterns of behaviour their directors decide upon. Computerised civilisation. No less. Manipulation of the mass-mind for purposes of the persuasive "people-planners".[24]

This process has to be applied at earliest infancy (or before), and continued during the "utility life" of the human units to be disposed of. To make this work effectively agents are needed, and the natural agency applicable during the first formative years and vitally essential "mind years" are schoolteachers who must necessarily conform to the selected "norm".

Much, if not all of this, may have already dawned on you. It does mean, however, that you are in the midst of a process yourself which is aimed entirely at conditioning your consciousness into precisely the state which the remote supervisors of the "Education authorities" intend shall be your attitude and outlook on life. You may suppose you were selected for your abilities or qualification or aptitudes etc, and so in part you were. The overriding factor deciding your selection for "teacher training" was that you that you must have seemed most likely to form suitable material for shaping into the sort of human unit currently required by the policy makers. Have you not noticed how "typecast" the teaching profession is becoming? At the moment you are going through a period of pressure which may literally bend your mind for many years ahead. These training

---

24 I don't think he got out much. All that went over my head at the time. I had no political awareness whatsoever and didn't understand the concept of left and right wings until I was in my 30s.

systems are not worked out by incompetents, and they are very well aware indeed of all the tricks of the mind-bending trade.[25]

You probably won't agree with any of this, and for all I know may resent my saying it. It wasn't a bit what you asked me for at all, and indeed I am seldom likely to react as requested. Never mind. No matter what you think, it will help, and what I <u>haven't</u> said will help still more in unexpected ways.

As for the third question, my "Inner Traditions of Magic" is probably most in your line. Anyway I hope it will help you. I've no news of further publications yet, owing to the Postal strike.

To understand Crowley, you had to know the man rather than his writings. It mildly amuses me when I note those of your generation make such a hopeless mess of interpreting anything he wrote, and finding meanings there he didn't even suspect himself. The "O.M." <u>must</u> be chortling his astral head off.[26]

Wm. G. Gray

---

25 It's a wonderful scenario but our tutors at the NCC were totally incompetent, and we as students were largely so. I went into teaching not for any altruistic motives but for the holidays. I was a rubbish teacher, and would not have wanted my children to be taught by me.

26 The 'Old Master' as they called Crowley.

14, Bennington St,
Cheltenham
Glos.

date as postmark.

Dear AR,

Well well! I do seem to have released cats in cotes.

If you check Mathers and old G.D. stuff, you'll find Michael in his right position.

As long as you realise you <u>are</u> being "processed" by your "Teacher's training", and that this <u>is</u> affecting your abilities of awareness, you know, or <u>should</u> know, enough to slide all this secondary conditioning of consciousness into the "Teacher-telesmic" you are building up to work with in this world, and BE WHAT AND WHOM YOU ARE otherwise as the Entity of your Self which you mean to endure through your incarnations in search of your True Identity. In making your "Teacher-telesmic" you should simply be making as useful a tool as possible to earn a living with in this life, not trying to force your Self into a form determined by the dictates of others. Of course this means living not a "double life", but on more than one level simultaneously.

So? Some day you will have to live on millions and more levels at once, but try two to start with. Everyone else has to. It doesn't mean you become two people. You simply fulfil several functions calling for distinct categories of consciousness.

What of the Tree? Isn't that a combination of ten entirely different categories of consciousness, each acting on its own, yet all totalling a whole Truth? So are we. So long as YOU stay "top-dog" of your own Self-System directing your various categories as Kether-Malkuth does, you'll come to no harm you can't deal with comfortably.

You certainly can't assume a Magical Identity by means of a Ring,[27] (or any other Key-Symbol) unless you have spent a very great deal of

---

27 He must have rattled me with that previous letter and I probably gave as tart a response as I dared. Also, I felt that by using a simple ring I could enable myself to switch from my normal sub-hippy persona into that needed to be an effective classroom teacher. I still think it is a good idea.

time and effort in building it up first. All any Symbol does, is help you "switch" from one Self-state to another IF you already have those Self-states available for your use. A switch is only useful if circuitry and a supply of power is also associated with it. Otherwise it is no more than a useless ornament screwed to a wall.

Your definition of Magic is rather good. One might perhaps improve it by suggesting that we evolve spiritually not by simply just copying "God characteristics", but by actually evoking our own characteristics of such a category out of our Nil-nucleus. Mere mimetic acts as such are not a lot of good. It is creative consciousness which counts.

I must confess I do rather agree with your tutor! One of the most important old GD disciplines was condensation and concentration of consciousness into focalised force all the while. Pages had to be reduced to paras, paras to sentences, sentences to syllables, and syllables to single Symbols. The end Symbol had to express the whole expanse it represented. Most of my quarrel with modern "pseud-thinking" is that it is confusional, illusional, and pollutional. A Zen roshi would have just one crude word for the lot: "Balls".

Once, Kung Fu Tze was accompanied by an earnest and well-meaning disciple during a nocturnal walk the sage had presumably intended for solitary meditation. The disciple flattered away about the Master's unique erudition and insight, saying that the duties of such a great soul to his fellow men for all time were surely to spend every possible moment writing down the Divine Wisdom for the guidance of posterity. Kung silently indicated with a finger all the Heavens above their heads and said completely and conclusively: "Does THAT write?"

Ask yourself this. In the interests of whom, what, or, to which category of consciousness is it, that Mankind should remain in a state of confusion, doubt, uncertainty, indecision, and mental muddle. Just why such subtle "people-programming" is pervading our so called "permissive" society. Permissive my foot! Real Inner freedoms are being curtailed and coerced on a scale never known before on earth. At one time there was a saying: "It's your money they're after." But now we have to add "And your mind above all." For what???? Why???? Who makes a profit out of it???? Whose loss of What???

"Initiation" means the awakening, bringing to Inner Light-Life, and emergence into Entity of an <u>Individual</u> worthy of seeking Selfhood in Ultimate Union with the Supreme Spirit. When we learn to live "Singly" to that Aim alone, then we may be fairly classified as "initiates" to at least some degree. Insofar as Magic serves this End, it is valuable. Otherwise it can be obstructional as with everything else.

As regards my books. If these and others of their vein don't result in either yourself or those of similar abilities writing a damn sight better ones when your turn comes round, (which it will), then a lot of us have wasted our lives in this idiotic world for nothing worth bothering with. Why else would we metaphorically get off our astral arses and pitch into action? I hope you have better and more encouraging responses than we've met with. Chances are you will, but don't take this for granted. Remember you lot have to take over where we leave off and carry the Tradition along another length of its life. Best wishes for your work.

Sincerely,

Wm. G. Gray

Good Friday

My Dear Alan

Thank you for your letter and SAE.

Your weather sounds worse than here. It is lifting today, so will hope for outing tomorrow.

Do you know, I just haven't a clue how to answer your question.[28]

Once, a young Zen student asked his instructor all about Heaven, Hell, the afterlife etc., and the teacher replied: I haven't the faintest idea whatever. The shocked young man ventured "But surely you are a Master of Zen and should know?" Reply was: "I'm not dead yet so how the Hell can I talk about what happens where I'm not?" A koan itself.

My answer is I can't tell you what I'm not told to. It won't help, but that's it.

Cussed, isn't it?

Good wishes for your holiday

Bill

---

28 I have no memory of what the question was. I was probably trying to show off.

My Dear Alan,

All right, I'm not going to preach, moralise, comment, or otherwise criticise. Why should I? Who the hell am I to adjudicate on the conduct of someone else's life after all the mistakes I've made with my own?

I'm not going to say I'm sorry your love-life blew up on you because that's a perfectly normal experience of living that most people go through in the course of an incarnation.

But I'm going to say I'm sorry if you let it affect you badly and deeply enough to cause adverse effects on your psyche that might take a long time to correct. You can actually make this into perhaps the most valuable experience of your young life which will do you all the good in the world and sort out a lot of your somewhat stuffy ideas for the better. Don't regret the happening – absorb it and build it into you constructively. I wish I'd known how to do this when the same thing happened to me some time before you were born to this "vale of tears". Don't think I don't know what happened to you. All that and much more was mine once. Like the old Abbé, "I survived" – and so will you, even better and more markedly.

I don't exactly know what ideas you had about the Path, but they seem oddly out of phase with its primal purpose – to develop and individualise an entity toward Divinity by means of living Initiation. What on earth makes you think that Life and Love, and Light don't go together???? They can't exist apart, being the chief concomitants of Cosmos.

OK. So you needed this experience like the rest of us, and it got dished out to you accordingly. You can thank your God it came during your present period of life, and not later on. It is the best possible time to happen.

Maybe your ideas of Love need adapting to actualities of Inner Life so that they fit better.

Balls to Alice Bailey, the pompous old prude. All these so-called "Great Mystics" make such a hopeless muck of their own love-lives it's just laughable. I wouldn't take their views too seriously if I were you.[29]

You have so much to learn so well worthwhile, and Life is doing its best to put you through all the drill on the Divine scale of manoeuvres for making Man into something more than merely mortal. Don't despair if its gets rough with you now and then. How else are You ever to succeed in being a Self worth Knowing????

Why should you "go back to your old ways"? Why not work out better ones with wider vision, more flexible forcefields and much finer methods???? Regrets are useless. Resolutions are far more practical.

Of course you got egoically hurt, but that's no reason why you should be spiritually harmed. There's a difference between the two types of damage. Actually the experience won't do you any harm whatever – indeed to the contrary – unless you deliberately allow this useless result. Strange to say, Life and its circumstances don't really hurt us at all, but we usually manage to hurt ourselves on account of what happens to us.

Think. <u>Who</u> has actually hurt you??? Or <u>what</u>, if you like? Life? God? Fate? The girl? Other humans? Or <u>have you really hurt yourself</u> because of maladjustment with these or other factors???? If so, you also have the power to heal yourself eventually. No one is denying that you have been hurt BUT, just where did that hurt originate from?????? Vital query.

If I acted logically, I'd congratulate you on passing through a very much needed experience expressly designed to improve your Cosmic chances of Individuation – but this sounds revoltingly hard-hearted and callous to anyone in your present condition of consciousness. What I will say instead, is that you haven't the least cause in the world for concern – little though you may suppose this now. In point of fact you had to have this experience in order to make you fit for further service in other spiritual areas. There was no other practical way for the "Powers that be" to open you up "livingly" so as to become more valuable for the purpose "behind you" in this and other incarnations.

What do you suppose "Initiation" means? A lot of impressively theatrical ceremonies? Secret services in strange Temples??? Such

---

29 In one of her books she had written about spirituality and sexuality being incompatible.

things are but symbols of actualities that have to be <u>lived</u> until you absorb them and integrate them into your Identity. There are all kinds of initiations, but Life, and the Spirit thereof, is the only genuine Initiating agency.

All right, Fine. So you've made a practical step on the Path of Life instead of a fanciful one. <u>Now</u> you can continue and get on with some real Lifework that matters. You can start being a genuine initiate instead of just an imaginary one. You did your rituals well, and obviously generated enough spiritual force to boot you into the one situation which would alter you into the sort of Self which other Selves on the same Path would welcome. Knowing, I believe you will be all the more pleased to make your own acquaintance with your Self as well. In other words your Magic <u>worked</u>, drastic as it might have seemed. YOU, your Real Self evoked your present Self-situation which the lesser part of your personality is now trying to cope with out of a very limited consciousness. This is a <u>good</u> thing per se, and it won't go bad on you unless you make a real balls of it by mismanagement – and I don't suppose you'll do that for a moment.

I don't know about your stars. Look here, send me your birth date, place, and <u>time of day</u> as accurately as you can. I'm not an astrologer, but my wife is. At least if I have a look at your chart we might get a clue at your characteristics. Oh no you won't get the chart, it would be purely for my private information, and it might help.

Forgive you? Good God whatever for?? Still, I can and do feel for you, but believe me you've nothing to forgive yourself for, and that's what really matters.

Best Wishes

Bill

Dear Alan Richardson,

I couldn't help a sympathetic smile over your last letter. I might have written it myself, more years ago than I care to admit. You certainly seem to be following along the same old true-tested pattern which must have come down almost Unchanged through the centuries. In years to come, you also will look at the young man you used to be in somebody else and smile with the rest of us all. It's a Life-pattern that none of us avoid who are going the same way.

Yet, – think, – <u>why</u> are you so very very anxious to find a mate??? Sex??? No, you can get that anyway. Companionship??? You can find that more easily apart from marriage. You won't like the fundamental reason at all, but sooner or later it will smack you in the face without much warning. What you are really seeking so desperately, is a life-partnership with a female human who might be capable of compensating your own deficiencies of Cosmic character, Somebody to fill up the holes in your Self, as one might say. Somebody who might do for you inwardly, what you should really do for yourself: You tell your "Person-self" that you seek a mate for spiritual rather than physical reasons – yes – so you do, <u>but</u> are these sound spiritual reasons???

In effect, you are more or less asking for someone else to get inside you and do your living for you along Inner lines of Life-Light you are Cosmically compelled to live your Self if ever you are to Individuate. You ask the Impossible of the Infinite. <u>No one</u> can <u>live</u> for you, any more than they might eat, drink, sleep, or fulfil any of your natural functions.

The Law is "BE AS THOU WILT". Not as anybody else wills, or as your purely personal and Pseudo-Self might wish during a momentary whim. No. The Will which made You as you Are and Will Be, in your very beginning, now, and until You end in AMEN. By expecting another Self to act in place of your true Identity, you ignore the Law of Inner Life, and so pay whatever penalty may be needed for compensation. This happens to us all, but to each according to instance. Sometimes called Karma.

So what do you, or anyone else, have to do about this Life-Law? Only one procedure is possible. Learn now to live so that you become able to bring out of your Self, whatever you are now expecting other Selves to push into you. This is a Live-it-your-Self Cosmos. Yet again, you will obtain your Self-supplies from others along a higher source. In simple terms, you get out of them from "God", what they put into "God" on their own accounts. We <u>do</u> obtain Self-supplies from each other, but it all depends <u>how</u> and <u>where from</u>. Don't expect to get love <u>directly</u> out of another human, for neither you, nor anyone else ever will, despite suppositions to the contrary. What you can and should expect to gain, is the love which other humans devote to their "Inner Infinities", which "bounces back" to <u>you</u> via your own Inner contacts with an Identity we all share and term "God" in such a variety of ways. Worked this way, the Cosmic circuit is complete, and Force-flows act accordingly. All this will take you a lifetime or so to catch up with, but it won't hurt to start considering the principles now, hard though this may sound.

It is not the pursuit of Magic that is lonely, but the pursuit of Life itself. You think that marriage might be an answer to what you are looking for? No man can be lonelier than when lying right beside a woman with whom he is unable to strike a single spark of Inner Light.

In this life you will not only have to learn how to be "alone" in your Self, but how to succeed spiritually with this process, so that you become an Individual Entity in your own right. A hard and tough lesson? Of course. It wouldn't be worth learning if it wasn't.

You are not looking for a mate really. You are looking for missing parts of your Self which you know "deep down" must be evolved. No mate could supply these, because you must grow them your Self on your own Tree. The seeds are there. Only when you have outgrown dependence on mate-seeking, are you likely to find one worth partnering while your respective lives run parallel for perhaps an incarnation.

Tough stuff. We have all had it thrown at us one way or another, and so far, you've come out of it better than many I might think of. You'll survive.

Good luck

Bill

51

July 24th 72

Dear Alan Richardson,

Many thanks for your letter and enclosed SAE.

Well, good, you are learning that you're learning! Of course Life is the Initiator. What else? And what do you live for? Individuation.[30]

By the time you have outgrown your first half dozen or so love affairs, you may be in a better position to look at Magic from perhaps a more practical view. It just gets bigger as you go along. So do you.

I would strongly advise you not to meet me. First because you would be deeply disappointed and disillusioned by my everyday personality and circumstances. It is always a mistake to meet people whose books you have valued. I know, because I've done it so often, and have given up this bad habit permanently, or at least the rest of this incarnation which won't be much longer now I should think. Second, because you won't meet the writer of those books anyway, only the outer crust of a man who typed them out and signed for them. And frankly that isn't really worth meeting. It's certainly crusty.[31]

Another thing, if I am to be honest, I have personally, (as me, Wm. G. Gray), got so bloody sick of all the various young people who have turned up out of curiosity, then turned tail when they realised I wasn't going to work the slightest miracle for them, that I do tend to look with very jaundiced eyes at any further visitors. Put at my crudest I've just about had a gut-full of the lot. That doesn't involve you personally of course, but it does mean you would only meet an old tired man with a prejudice against probing people.

The other day I came across a wonderful "hippy" poster. It said:
WHEN THE LAST SOCIOLOGIST IS STRANGLED WITH THE GUTS OF THE LAST POLITICIAN, THERE'LL STILL BE PROBLEMS, BUT IT'LL BE A GOOD START ANYWAY.

---

30 I was feeling grown up because my new flame Sian B had been two-timing me and I finished with her.
31 In kabbalistic terms he was, by own admission, a Geburah figure with all the traditional Vices and Virtues of this sphere – though he might not have liked you pointing out the former.

That's more or less how I feel about people in general after a lifetime of living with them.

If you still insist on seeing me, come entirely at your own risk and responsibility, providing I know precisely when to expect you, but don't say you weren't warned, and you would be wisest to steer clear. Otherwise you are welcome.

Good wishes for your future.

Wm. G Gray

14, Bennington St,
Cheltenham.
Glos. GL50 4ED
Tel 24129

Aug 2nd 72

Dear Alan Richardson,

OK. OK. Come along then, but NOT before 7.30 pm. I work till about six, and then eat. Did you ever try visiting a bear with a sore head while it was trying to have its honey??? No? After 7.50 I assume human shape after a fashion and rarely go to bed before midnight.

Just at the moment I'm at a slack period with one book just completed, and nothing particular contemplated beyond very ordinary humdrum routine stuff. So I do have time for a little relaxation till the next spasm.

OK, 15th, Tues, 7.50.

Yes, do come on your own, I promise not to eat or ill-treat you. I've had so much of this: "May I bring my friend?" lark, and it's a dead waste of time and temper. They bring their friends who are bored stiff, or like fishes out of water, or can't stand the smell of incense, or allergic to cats, or just plain think I stink or what have you. You name it, I've had it. Now my firm rule is: NO FRIENDS or enemies for that matter. If they want to see me, they can bloody well ask for themselves and we'll take it from there.

Incidentally I look much more like Aleister Crowley than Gandalf and I didn't like either of them, especially the former, though he was more like a little boy than a BIG BEAST.

Sincerely,

Wm. G. Gray

14, Bennington St,
Cheltenham.
Glos. GL50 4ED

Aug 31st 72

Dear Alan Richardson,

Will pass your letter on to Norman when I see him next.[32] His concern is probably due to the fact he has a son about your age and therefore really is involved with the future of the next generation. I wouldn't guarantee a reply though; he is an exceptionally hardworking man with almost every second committed somewhere. I know he will be very touched and pleased you wrote to him though, and if I know him, will rather treasure your letter. His arrival was purely fortuitous by the way, I hadn't a clue he was coming and in fact never do know in advance. You put up a very good show against numbers, though no one was attacking your generation.[33]

The comic thing is that every generation says the same things, and nothing will convince them it hasn't been said before. Each group of youngsters think they have invented sex. God knows what they think we did at their age apart from fighting in idiotic wars for damn all that mattered. Even the slang is medieval. I watch young people get more and more old fashioned every day in fact. Clothes that were out of date when my mother was a girl. It is really rather funny. All people ever do is the same old silly things in another variety of ways. In the end it gets so monotonous one dies out of sheer boredom.[34]

This is one main factor that attracts young folk to Magic. Because it is so old yet ever new, because it offers them what this world doesn't – Hope. It offers them another gift they have lost – Love. It

---

32 Norman Gibbs. I had an incredible sense of instant recognition, linked with Roman times.
33 I argued that my generation weren't too bad. Norman was deeply concerned. Bill stuck up for the hippies, arguing that they acted like damping rods in a nuclear reactor, and if it wasn't for them the whole world would blow up into total war all over again. I think he was right.
34 I now hear myself saying exactly the same.

might make Life worthwhile, except just a grind in more senses than one. It might even offer a breath of fresh air from the corruption of this world. No wonder they seek it.

Oh yes, one thing I can say to you which possibly nobody else would, and it is meant to <u>help</u> you maybe more than you might think. I noted you had a strong North Country accent. There's nowt against that, but it will cost you your hopes of all the best jobs. Nobody would tell you why either. Interview boards would deny this emphatically, but at the same time they would "select" other candidates with maybe less qualifications.[35] The thing to do is invest in a cassette tape recorder, listen to yourself, and go on practising elocution until you get a "standard" result. Believe me, this could make a very big difference to you. Coming from me, you needn't give a damn, whereas from anybody else you might be offended.

Good luck anyway. If you come this way again, contact.

35 Bill was right about those accents in those days. As a result of his advice my own today is a ridiculous mish-mash that some think is Irish. Now, a regional accent is treasured.

Mar 2nd

Dear Alan,

Glad you got back OK. Best of luck.

Your Query is reasonable, but I had an idea I'd covered it already somewhere. Although <u>theoretically</u> everyone ought to be a perfect balance of the Qualities in themselves, we just aren't as human beings, and that's all about it. Now this means that usually everyone has dominant qualities in some direction or other, and usually deficient qualities in the opposite direction. In other words we tend to have spiritual "specialities" as "Cosmic characteristics" which are usually alignable with one of the Quarters in particular. One might even call them "Imperfects" because of preponderance in that sector. So, what to do is select four of these "Imperfects" so that between them they balance out into making an harmonious whole, or "gestalt" used to be the "In" word. They balance <u>because</u> of their association into a "Magic Circle". So it works. <u>If</u> (and I'd surely like to meet this) one could find a perfectly balanced person, they would never need a Circle at all, since they would be that very thing themselves. Actually the Circle member who needs to be best balanced is the Cord.

A typical "Cup-person" as you put it, would simply mediate their own natural qualities of kindness, sympathy, love, and cheerfulness through themselves into the Circle. Granted the others would have a proportion of such qualities in themselves (one hopes), but with the Cup they would be outstanding. For instance, I am deficient in all those qualities, therefore cannot supply them. Neither can Bobbie, nor in fact anyone we know suitable for inclusion in the Circle except someone too far away to partake. A sad admission maybe, but there it is. As it is not only futile but also damaging to go on working with an unbalanced circle (like trying to run a car with one wheel off, and passengers leaning frantically to one side hoping to keep the thing on an even keel till the brakes work safely) I thought it best to close up altogether. Have no intention of reopening unless and until a suitable Cup comes along, which probably won't happen at all this incarnation.

Does that clear up your problem???

I'm having my customary karmic publisher trouble again. It gets very discouraging. They are obviously going to make a cheap nasty and rotten production of my masterpiece "The Rite of Light" with IBM unjustified, all the wrong typefaces, and God knows what rubbishy cover, that I'm trying to get the contract cancelled and get money back to call it off altogether. The bastards are <u>butchering</u> the work. I've managed to get the "Rollright Ritual" away from them because it wasn't typeset, and no money had been paid down. Somebody else will take it some time. The "Self Made by Magic" I cant stop them bringing out. It's paid for, typeset, and God knows what they are doing with it. It would be heart-breaking if I had a heart left to break. I've got feelers out hopefully to other publishing houses, but not really a lot of great hope.

Good God, take Francis Regardie. You'd think publishers would be glad to have his stuff, wouldn't you??? He has ceased bothering any more. Llewellyns have done him out of probably 320,000 dollars reprinting all his early stuff with no copyright. He hasn't had a cent. Dion Fortune had to pay for her own (she could afford it) and Crowley beggared himself paying for publications that have since made fortunes for pirates. As Regardie said recently to me, "The bloody Gods haven't helped us a bit!" and neither have they, so far as I can see.

So, whatever you do, don't expect any kind of "gratitude" from any sort of "God" if you would enter the Magical arena of Life. You won't get it. Learn not to depend on Divinity for <u>anything</u> whatever. Do what you are called to do <u>out of yourself</u> because that particular something is yours to do and nobody else's. But for God's sake (the God in you, that is) don't expect any pay-off or rewards therefrom. Take what comes if and when it comes, and that's that.

Come to think of it brutally, what did Jesus of Nazareth ever gain personally from his work? Misunderstanding, ill-treatment, insults, torture, ignominious death. What have his exploiters gained? Untold millions of money, whole countries, you name it they've got it. If you look at those nearer our time, what have they to show?

The deeper you would go into Magic, the more dedicated you have to be in order to survive the spiritual stresses and sheer adversities that will come against you from all Quarters. The Instruments are well called "Weapons", you will need them all to fight for your very life and existence as pressures mount almost insupportably. Once you get past the surface stuff, you will come up against the really tough trials and grimness that underlies everything. Through that again, of course, comes PEACE, but scarcely without a struggle to attain it.

It is odd (maybe) but my two works mainly written in direct opposition to Evil per se, have just about had everything done to prevent publication, and the next few weeks will determine what happens. One organisation in USA (not Sangreal) are willing to handle them if discount is favourable enough, but I don't know about their distribution abilities. I feel there is a "make-or-break" point very imminent.

Oh well, enough of my troubles. Of course stop by in the summer. So far as I know, we aren't going anywhere.

No, I'm not writing another damn thing in my life unless I get what's on my hands shifted along somewhere. In fact my writings have caused me so much personal unhappiness, frustration, inconvenience, loss, and sheer animosity in all directions, I rather wish to God I hadn't set pen to paper (metaphorically) They haven't even made any money worth having either. Nor will while I'm alive.

So, be very sure of yourself before seeking entry to the "Inner arenas", and don't say you weren't warned. Once in, there's no turning back. One has to go on, and on, and on, to the bitter bloody end, because one has to. No matter how horrible, how frustrating, or more frequently how blatantly boring the Inner Path may seem, it has to be plodded to the very final and sometimes terrible end before it enters PEACE PROFOUND wherein Nothing can harm or hurt you ever again. You can't just "take up Magic" like some hobby and abandon it when you feel inclined. You may, and periodically should, have "resting" periods during which nothing much appears on the surface while a good deal is developing underneath. Nevertheless, once you become part and parcel of the Magical Tradition, especially that of the West, expect difficulties from all directions. Ultimately you will either overcome or outlive them, even if you re-incarnate a few lives on the way.

Most people get "attracted to Magic" because they think they can get a lot of something for nothing. Once they find that in fact the exact opposite is true, and one has to give up everything to gain

59

Nothing, this frightens them off sharpish. Only those with the sheer Cosmic courage and "long-lighted" spiritual sight can pass the Inner point of peril that topples reason into ruin and ambition into the Abyss. It's the old story of many being called, and few, so few, being chosen.

Well, I guess that's just about it for this session. Prolonged typing plays my arthritic wrist up a bit these days.

All the best for now,

Wm f. fray,

14, Bennington St,
Cheltenham
Glos.

date as postmark.

Dear Alan Richardson,

Sex Magic.[36] No I'm not going to sit down and write a long dissertation on "Sex Magic" which might sell as an article or book-chapter. Let's face its facts.

1. Where, and much more rarely when, any genuine "Sex Magic" is purely for one purpose. Breeding. i.e. selection of specific souls for embodiment, be these Good or Evil.

2. The vast majority of so-called Sex Magic is no more than psychological window-dressing for kicks, i.e. for the benefit of those who like sex in fancy dress or with party whips, or what have you. Largely this stems from guilt-inadequacy factors, or whatever makes people disguise motives from themselves and each other. Psychologically this may be a fascinating study or come up with some comical answers, but it all boils down to the same thing – fun or fear fantasies enjoyed by employers.

3. Much of primitive "Sex Magic" amounted to elementary birth and population control proceedings. i.e. copulation with inanimates or other forms of masturbation. Motives were simply those of tension-reliefs coupled with symbolic acts of consciousness for the sake of psychological satisfaction. In other words, humans always seek justification or excuses for their conduct.

4. Because early diets were so poor in vitamins and scanty in quantity, most primitives suffered greatly with malnutrition especially in

---

36 I had devised a turgid 'Moonchild-y' ritual involving all sorts of phallic kabbalistic symbolism: rods, cups etc. I also sent it to Aossic, expecting he would immediately grant me Grand Mastership of the OTO. Bewilderingly, he suggested (again) that I might want to do 9 months of real Work first.

fertility-productive agents. They could only compensate for this in some measure by elaborate ritual procedures for "working themselves up" into a procreative mood. They, like their animals, were seasonal breeders. What is most important to remember, psychologically they needed a lot of stimulation and encouragement, which was where the "Magic" came in. What about nowadays, when so many have to have their pet "thing" whatever it may be, before they achieve competence in copulation? You'd be amazed at the variety, and even at my age, I'm still hearing new and even sillier ones. That's Sex Magic up to date.

Just why, in the Name of God can't you accept a sex relationship with a woman for one valid Magic reason only. The best one. That you love her as a person and she likewise loves you? If you haven't anyone you love, then satisfy your physical sex-needs with whatever won't hurt anyone, and happens to fulfil your psychological lacunae. One important thing. It is a terrible spiritual responsibility to drag other souls into incarnation in this world. Especially in this era. The careless indifference with which people recklessly reproduce their species is scarcely short of criminal. In these contraceptive times there is no excuse whatsoever for such irresponsibility. So, unless you are grimly determined to make some other soul share this earthly environment with you, or feel quite certain you have Inner authorisation for such sponsorship, and what is most of all, are fully prepared to fulfil the obligation, don't force fathership on yourself or unplanned pregnancy on the wretched girl.

That is why celibacy was enjoined on initiated priesthood in olden times. It wasn't that any particular virtue lay in celibacy itself, but in the fact that unborn souls of that grade were not brought into unnecessary incarnation by careless copulation.

What would happen if you tried your Sex Magic idea? Damned if I know, except your girl would probably go off the boil, and you, at the same time. Sounds like one of those Tantric things that take half the night and everybody's lost interest before it's half way through. Why not just enjoy the thing and each other as an act of mutual affection??? Or if that proves impossible, relieve tensions by some harmless means.

I'm afraid I've seen and heard so much bloody rubbish masquerading as Sex Magic, that I'm just about disenchanted with the topic. I think of the great Aleister Crowley sitting up in bed casting I

Ching sticks to decide whether or not he wakes Leah up to poke her or not. I think of skinny old Gerald Gardner, King (?) of the Witches prancing around with elk-horns from a coat-rack tied on his head while the girls tickle his tool with a pink feather duster. I think of all these so-called Master Magicians and High Priests of Witch Covens living on National Assistance and trying to convince themselves they are Adepts and God knows what of Sex Magic when they couldn't even raise a good fart between the lot – let alone anything more dangerously fertile. All because of a pathetic puerility and a lack of genuine love anywhere. Poor, poor little people. God grant them love in their next life-rounds. They need it desperately.

About Thorsons. A slimy lot of catchpennies. Watch you don't get caught on their filthy contract trick of 10% of publishers profits on bulk sales abroad, plus keeping copyright and a lot of other seamy little tricks to trap the unwary.[37] They pay out more promptly than they did. For myself, I'm financing my own work for the next four books and see what happens. One is supposed to come out before Christmas, the most important one in Jan, another next Midsummer, and one typing up now probably next Christmas. Another effort is being printed now in USA, plus one section of a special for California University possibly in print maybe two years. Financial profit about nil, because they will pay for each other, and whatever they produce goes to more new work while I live. After that profits if any, go to widow.

By the way, all that balls about: "I desire to know in order to serve" is purely Inner Light interpretation. But note it doesn't say serve what or whom, does it???? There's nothing to stop anyone saying that aloud, then carrying on in their own minds for the rest of the sentence. Is there? I'm afraid the phrase rather stuck in my gullet when I said it, and never mind what I added after it under my breath.

Oh well. That's it I guess for the nonce.

---

37 I had already written by hand what much later became my first book, the clunkingly entitled *Introduction to the Mystical Qabalah* which eventually came out in 1974. They gave me 2%.

about the 8th Nov I think.

Dear Alan,

I'm writing by reply because I appreciated your letter so much on account of its sheer honesty and sense of true values. That is scarcer than hens' teeth with most of the crappy correspondence I now simply chuck in the waste basket. Oh yes, you'll get your quota of this if you ever get anything published. Take my tip and do the same when it arrives. However, it does make one value the odd genuine contact all the more.

Of course your letters don't offend me. Why the hell should they? I'm simply trying to repay an old "Karmic" debt in a way. When I was your age I used to write all my "occult" problems to someone who was about what my age and experience now is to you. I certainly couldn't have discussed them with my own father. Anyway, I got dealt with fairly bluntly on many occasions, and it helped. Even to this day I remember my old "teacher" in commemorations of the dead. So if I've managed to help you (I hope) it goes back to him also, and the line he came from. Do the same when your turn comes, (which it will), and so pass on whatever there may be to pass.

There's no reason in all the world why you shouldn't be interested in the methods and mechanics of sex, magical or otherwise. It would be more than odd if you weren't. Nor is there any particular reason to bother a lot about what may or may not turn others on. Everyone has their "thing" one way or another. Providing it doesn't hurt or upset others intentionally, there isn't any real harm done. (Or much magic either, except insofar as psychological necessities may be considered magic.)

Good Lord, I didn't say there was anything exactly wrong with Gardner's games. All I can do is go into fits of laughter at the solemn silliness of the picture. As farce it is priceless, but as "Witchcraft" or "Magic" only absurd. It's only a question of values really.

There's one point you younger lot ought to keep in mind when reflecting on the peculiarities of past generations. For quite a period, sex was something entirely and absolutely "under the counter". Nobody spoke of it openly, the topic was considered shameful, the

64

vaguest allusions to it were shocking, and people tried to live as if it wasn't there. This gave rise to some very odd attitudes and actions. It also accounted for much, if not all of the mental misunderstandings on the subject. Look, do an odd science-fictiony extrapolation. Imagine a society in which nobody admitted eating. Food could only be bought furtively and secretively, carefully concealed, consumed behind locked doors, never mentioned except allusively, considered shameful, and all the rest of it. Sex on the other hand was something everybody did quite cheerfully in parties or quite naturally with each other. Imagine secret societies gathered in locked lodges to celebrate the disgusting practice of cooking and actually eating. See them leering over the consecrated frying pan with its loathsome and suffocating fumes of eggs and b----n (Ugh!) Develop this fantasy a bit, and see what it reveals of the psychology of sex-magic as applied to earlier generations. Moral? Forbidden fruit is always tastiest! I once thought of how to stop sex altogether – Nationalise it and make it compulsory! In the end you'd have to give double Green Shield stamps before anyone would do it at all.

Most of the "magic" to sex of past times lay with its forbiddeness. Few aphrodisiacs work better.

I'm glad to hear you love someone, and I hope maybe you will find some happiness together in this tragic world. That really would be a wonderful magic. One well worth passing on too.[38]

Of course you get a "de-glamorise magic" period. Everyone does. All you actually de-glamorise of it are your own mistaken ideas. Out of that you go on to reach realities you'll grow into quite naturally and simply. It's like a child losing interest in toys as it grows into concern with tools. Later in life of course it comes to realise how important its toys really were.

In point of fact, you've already done a bloody sight better with your magical experiences than many do in a whole lifetime. All it did for Crowley for instance was impoverish and ruin him because he misused it from lack of experience and judgement, although it must be admitted his own parents had a lot to answer for on account of attitudes to sex, while they in their turn were part of a preconditioned system.

---

38 Well, Laura also two-timed me and kept us both on a string for a long time, though t'other guy didn't know I existed! We're still friends today though, after her apology to me 40 years later.

You mustn't forget however, that though modern attitudes seem so "permissive" in relation to sex, this is actually an illusion, and mentalities are being just as ruthlessly warped and exploited in other ways by "mind-benders". Though previous generations may have been so proscribed and peculiar in sex-fields, they were actually far freer in emotional and empathic areas than most moderns who are being "computer conditioned" to conform with a predictable political and commercial pattern for very big buyers. Remember that sex these days is a selling agent and the key to multimillion dollars enterprises. That's all it's worth to its biggest prostituters. Look for the keys of evil where money and power concentrate most, and there you'll find them lying. Remember too, that not one would turn in any lock if humans weren't so greedy, stupid, vain, and vicious. If a lifetime of school-mastering doesn't put you off humans for good, nothing will.

Anyway, good luck and good wishes.

Dear Alan,

First congratulations on passing your final teaching practice, and best wishes for your future thereat. If you make the Bristol area we might be seeing something of you on account of it being but a local bus ride so to speak. It is an odd fact maybe, but those whom I call serious occultists all steadily gravitate to the westward areas of these isles. Very quietly and unobtrusively, but definitely.

Well now let's take your $64,000 question.[39] You do manage to put your finger on salient issues and ask pertinent questions. Let's hope you get equally bright children in your own classes to give you some necessary encouragement from time to time.

First, I think you are expecting higher standards of all those people than they ever deserved or maybe supposed themselves. Who exactly said they were front runners in our evolutionary progress???? They were in fact extremely outreaching, specialised with only <u>part</u> of themselves, balancing the rest very precariously on a wobbly pedestal of ambition. In a sense, they were more or less like someone who had climbed a somewhat shaky ladder in pursuit of a glittering objective which they only managed to brush with the tips of wildly waving fingers while hanging on with extremities of toes and the other hand. What can anyone in such a position actually do? They may perceive the outside of their pursued prize, talk and guess at and about it, perhaps describe their sensory impressions and opinions. In other words, alert the attention of those lower on the ladder, but that is about all. Intelligence doesn't give people good qualities, sound judgement, or basic characteristics necessary for sound and sensible dealings with metaphysical actualities. Intellectual brilliance has never been synonymous with <u>genuine</u> sanctity and true spirituality.

Dion Fortune was crammed with human faults she was very well aware of indeed, and if you called Francis Regardie anything wonderful he'd promptly say "Arseholes" in his best Cockney-American, or maybe more. He can be very colourful when he tries.

---

39 Having been reading Francis King's histories about the Magical Orders in Britain, I wondered why the Adepts acted like such idiots if they were in contact with Higher Powers.

What I specially love with him is his 100% sincerity and complete down-to-earth disdain of pretentiousness. We can call each other all the old bastards we feel like and enjoy it immensely.

You are looking at all the rubbish and crap connected with Mathers et al, and naturally it shocks you because you had a much better opinion of them which you now have to alter. In other words your own idealism has had a bit of a blow, and that's what bothers you. It happens to all of us, and better sooner than later. You asked for more, dear Oliver, than was in the cauldron to offer you. These people were not and are not saint-hero-figures of nobility, virtue, honour, or anything look-uppable to. They happened to be common-or-garden humans like the rest of us, but with a specially extended Inner faculty of apperception in areas otherwise relatively unused by majority-mankind. That did not automatically make them better people, but only different people. Give them a few incarnations to sort things out, and you may hear another story.

Oh yes, they made a mess of their personality-projections like you might make a mess of some theatrical part. Millions do far worse than that, but you notice these few because they were operative in a main area of your interests. If you are looking for hero-saint figures you certainly won't find them in most magical fields of action.

Oddly enough, you will find in folk-mythology myriad instances about what seems a very petty side of otherwise grand people. You should read some of the stories current about Jesus as a young man still extant in Middle Eastern tradition. All show him as someone of quick temper very difficult to control and with an extremely deep sense of injustice. The milk-and-water Jesus of the Gospels doesn't come into it at all. Only the raid on Temple money-changers, and cursing a barren fig-tree show anything of the Jesus his own people remember.

Under extreme spiritual pressures, faults and weaknesses show up in everyone. This happens with people like Mathers and others who invoke energies their own constructions are unable to withstand. It is inevitable. If people jump out of windows they will fall to the ground, and if they arouse Inner energies they can't equate out, then worse happens. Have you ever tried connecting the mains to your transistor set???? An expensive way of demonstrating this point.

How to avoid the same mistakes? All anyone can do is work on themselves to build up accurate Inner circuitry for dealing with the energies intended to be invoked, and don't generate the power until the pile is properly prepared. How do you activate an atomic pile? Construct it first so that it will dissipate more energy than is needed, then activate it <u>at a rate</u> which is well within safety limits. Otherwise you have an unwanted atomic bomb blast, don't you??? Same rules exactly apply in Magic. Make your Circle-cyclotron first, then activate it next. Learn from the failures of previous practitioners. Now then, think of this. Suppose – as indeed seems possible – the lives of Mathers and other muck-merchants provided yourself and others with lessons which meant you could succeed where they failed; would those lives have been entirely wasted???? You see as my own old "teacher" used to say: "Blame none for making mistakes, but blame everyone who refuses to learn from them."

In any case, most of this so-called "blasting" is either exaggerated bragging or a certain amount of plain balls. Most of the time it was "coming to them anyway" and a vociferous ill-wisher just claims the credit. Anyway the "witches" I know couldn't curse a fly to death at half an inch range. Me, for instance, I'll curse like Hell down at personal level and promptly cancel the lot higher up. So why do it at all? Equation of energy which would otherwise build up toward dangerous critical mass. Crude maybe, but rapidly effective, and relatively harmless.

Now if I could curse with any deadly effect, I'd be sorely tempted to blast Aquarian publication for the cheap dirty crooks they are. Unhappily I'd have to call that curse on myself also for sheer stupidity and gullibility due to lack of knowledge about the deep dirt in the publication game. I bought the knowledge the dear way. The moral is, never, never, NEVER sign a contract or even a sheet of bog-paper without either expert knowledge or getting a solicitor to vet it first. Here are this year's sales figures just received, and I'm still spitting a feather or two:

Seasonal Occult Rituals. 438 copies.
Inner Traditions of Magic. 520 copies. [40]

You will reckon that the shop price of all this literature comes to £1,827. Now how much of this do I, the author get for all the years

---

40 Far better sales than my books!

work they took to write???? I'm almost ashamed to write it. The princely, magnificent, super-colossal sum of £94.00. I assure you, I'm looking at the cheque right now with hate. So where does the rest go? Why does the publisher have a Rolls while I have a bicycle? Yet why curse him when my own stupidity is at fault? What actually happens of course is that they bulk-sale the lot abroad on which they pay hardly any commission at all, then get back fringe benefits from USA houses working the same racket over here. So why didn't my "Inners" warn me? They did a long time back. Said quite plainly there would be no immediate reward whatever for anything I did in this world, others would get the benefit, and anyway by the time anything interesting did turn up I'd be too old to care a damn in any case. So what the Hell made me go on with such a thankless, profitless, and seemingly pointless piece of Inner work??? Maybe you can answer that one for <u>me</u>, because I'm still wondering.

Anyway I reckon that's about enough for one day. I understand about your parents, but probably most of it sprang from maybe clumsy concern for you in case you wasted your time, failed your studies, and generally messed up your life. Probably it came from anxiety about you they couldn't put into words. The day may come when your own kids will bother you with whatever is the equivalent of Hippiedom or "generation revolt" in their days of teenage terrification. Every wave of youth thinks it is the one and only, etc. My own mother was "in the Tradition" herself, but my father hated it. So I can see both sides. Keep going. Once you get your job settled and routined up you can start expanding a bit.[41] Don't try to be like any other occultist whatever.

BE WHAT IS IN YOU and nobody else.

Best Seasons greetings and so forth.

Bill

Bill

---

41 Before I started my first teaching job in Gloucester, 1973, I spent several happy months working as a Nursing Auxiliary again at a mental hospital in Barrow Gurney. I knew that I was about to face one of the worst years of my life. Not so much expanding as imploding.

Dear Alan,

A typewriter is a purchase you never regret. I had my first one when I was 14. It cost me 7/6d second hand and it took me days to get working. A Yost with 48 separate keys. No ribbon, but an inking pad. You couldn't see what you typed because it worked from underneath, but the carriage could be lifted to see what happened. About ten lines later of course it appeared round the roller. I've still got a few bits I did with it then. Sentiment. My present machine I use all the time is about 60 years old, an American Remington portable from the days when they really made good models. It was old when I got it thirty years ago. I'll give you one useful tip, always back your paper with about three other sheets between it and the platen. That way, the extra thickness acts as a sort of shock-absorber and the platen lasts very much longer. So does the typeface. This type you are reading now is about 60 years old. You'll soon pick up speed. I hate to confess this, but I still type with two fingers after all these years because I didn't learn typing properly. Don't fall into the same error if you can help it. At any rate I type as fast as I can compose my thoughts to be put down on paper, and that suits me fine.

Now your queries (what I can do with a few words). By and large the "Lesser" Mysteries are the synthetic symbolisations of the "Greater" actualities of awareness and action they represent. The "Lesser" lead to the "Greater" much as for instance childhood leads to adulthood. Yet get the first right and the second works out well in consequence. You, as a teacher for instance, are supposed to train younger folk in the "Lesser" lessons which will enable them to fulfil their functions in the "Greater" spheres of living outside school conditions. Substitute Lodge or Temple for school, and you can see how things work. Yet it is easy to mistake the meaning of "Lesser" in terms of belittlement, which should never be done. If anything, the so called "Lesser" is of more importance in one sense than the "Greater", because it is only in and with the "Lesser" that we become able to cope adequately with the "Greater" when we have to handle ourselves livingly on those higher levels. Perhaps it links with an old theatrical saying. There are no "big" or "little" parts. Only well or badly played ones. Don't for God's sake look at most group leaders for examples except maybe awful ones. You are in the Mysteries of Life to BE YOURSELF and nobody else.

Avatars are "humans plus". They do not lead into spheres of no Collective Consciousness, although truly it may not be the collective Consciousness of <u>Mankind</u>. There <u>are</u> other than merely mortal minds operative in this Universe you know, our Avatars are only going somewhat ahead of the human mainstream into Inner areas already well worked by types of Awareness much in advance of ours. We are not <u>quite</u> such clever little creatures as we would like to suppose. What looks void and meaningless to us appears totally different to consciousness operating along frequencies we cannot begin to reach from brain-embodiment levels. What seems to <u>us</u> Nothing, Nil, Infinite Impossibility, etc; is quite otherwise with those whose familiar conditions it happens to be. Hence the importance of Zero. Zero to <u>us</u>, but not necessarily to who or what takes their Zero at some point far deeper than ours. And so on.

Oh yes, my next books. Only to-day I've sent corrected proofs back of "A Self Made by Magic". I'm narked because they've left this unjustified right margin to pages for the sake of economy. Shows silly corner-cutting that looks bad. Otherwise the type (photolith of course) looks good enough. In theory the book should be produced about Xmas, later than originally planned but just scraping into contract time.

They are not privately printed, but by cost sharing between me and publishers. They should be available through the ordinary bookshops and distribution channels eventually, but in case of difficulty write to publishers direct:

Janay Publishing Co Ltd,
60, North St,
Chichester
Sussex.

The next book, "The Rite of Light", is a magico-religious work of a complete Magical Mass which has taken a lifetime to co-ordinate. Proofs of that should come in a few weeks at most. The Church of

Hermetic Science in Pasadena are doing a special Christmas Mass using this Rite they tell me. I am only sorry I cannot celebrate it for them. Of course it won't be published till maybe Feb I should think. There were certain elements that tried to stop it being published altogether. Nothing remotely like it has ever reached print yet.

"The Rollright Ritual" is quite different, being Stone Circle working. I've just got the typescript of the "Tree of Evil" away but will need to raise finance to get it printed. Did you know, by the way, that both Dion Fortune and Crowley had to pay for all their books to be published originally? Now the sharks are reprinting them for pure publishers' profits with impunity. Fortune could afford it. She was connected with Firth stainless steel. Crowley virtually beggared himself in the end trying to pay printers. No bookseller would touch his stuff. I haven't a brass farthing I haven't earned by sweat blood and tears, and bloody little to show at the end of a virtually penniless lifetime. All I can do is publish from profits of first books so that in fact they don't make a penny piece for my personal use beyond cost of materials and actual basic expenses.

Publication is a hell of an expensive hobby. Even doing it on a shared subscription basis costs about £380 for an average book to the author. Some firms want more. This means that author and publishers have to sell at least 800 books to barely get their money back. After that of course is profit. The main problem is distribution and marketing. In point of fact, the best and bulk of sales for my type of stuff comes from mail order lists, believe it or not. Sales are very slow, but quite steady, going on for many years after the author has died. Look at Dion Fortune's stuff. It probably sells better now than when she was alive. Why? Because it's genuine. How much of the crap churned out by hacks ever survives another edition?

Another question to ask yourself. Just how many what I call real occult books have been published in the last few years???? The "occult explosion" is a myth invented by publishers to launch rubbish on the market. Do you sometimes have a strange feeling that the mass-media is quite willing to "get the occult a bad name" one way or another???? You could be right. Now ask yourself why and see what you come up with.

Do you want an interesting project? Get hold of Kenneth Grant's latest "Magical Revival" by Muller (this year) from local library, and having read it, write me your honest <u>feelings</u> about it. <u>Not</u> an intellectual analysis, but your deep-down feelings as to its worthiness or otherwise <u>as something likely to influence young people</u> who are looking for fundamental realities in "Magical " areas. Don't ask me why or wherefore just now. First tell me, then afterwards I'll explain. I just don't want to impede your critical faculties one way or another. O.K. This <u>could</u> be important. See what you can do.

Good wishes.

Bill Gray.

Norman Gibbs who has just dropped in (whom you might remember) would like to send you his kind regards also.

Dear Alan,

Your comments re K. Grant's M. Revival are of great interest insofar as they indicate reactions. It is taken that your general conclusions are that it wouldn't do you much good. Of course you seem to be judging intellectually rather than with Inner instinct, which does make a barrier.

In point of fact, the book is one of the <u>nastiest</u> and most seriously spiritually damaging works printed in this century. And NOT on account of the sex-themes. Something far deeper and dirtier than any simplicity of sex could ever be. The sex is purely a "lead-in" to the really vicious stuff, much as relatively harmless "pot" may grease the slide to soul-destroying heroin and the like. Where the truly "deep evil" comes in, lies with persuading people to abrogate or "hand-over" their own spiritual integrity, (and consequently every power and potential in them) into the grasping clutches of "entities" whose interests are quite opposite to our best and highest possibilities as humans.

Let us put it in simple child-terms (which are often the best.) Take it that we are mortal humans who are able to evolve and emancipate altogether away from Earth-incarnation limitations into far finer and more spiritually satisfactory forms of Life in terms of what would seem now to us pure energy and non-carnal consciousness. That is (or should be) our Life-aim. "Magic" but one method of assisting it.

Now either we advance this "Magnum Opus" or retard it. It is an individual effort for each entity. There <u>do</u> exist those that have no intention of any such "self-sacrifice" whatever, because they prefer existence in the force-frameworks of "worlds" like ours. That kind of living, however, demands continual supplies of energy from whatever source is most practically convenient. On this Earth, the simplest supply-source is from humans who are virtually willing to "hand over on a plate" absolutely enormous amounts of Inner energy in return for "spin-offs" after conversion into profits directed quite away from humanity's highest possibilities. Years ago this was called "selling one's soul to the Devil", but describe it in any terms you like it amounts to the same thing.

Without getting too involved, this is exactly what K. Grant's book encourages readers to do. Direct their spiritual energies into "pick-up points" where they can be neatly looted by collectors along those lines. From almost every viewpoint it's a pretty offensive piece of work. What I would call <u>real</u> pornography, i.e. "intended to corrupt and deprave."

Mind you, the principles behind this go on all the time everywhere in our world. Corruption of Church-State leadership has always been with us. Perhaps one should say "Church-State-Commerce" as a triad of People-pushers. Maybe these days "Commerce-State-Computer" might be more accurate. Whatever operates the three Pillars of the Tree of Evil – Compulsion, Coercion and Condemnation. So long as spiritual aspirants realise the existence of these "Evil Three", and learn to live otherwise, that's all to be done. Whether ill-willers are incarnate or discarnate doesn't make much difference to the principles concerned – only to focal fields.

You have to remember Dion Fortune was brought up at a time when sex was almost the ultimate sin, and masturbation was so utterly outrageous you didn't dare <u>think</u> it aloud. Penalties for tool-tinkering ranged from eternal Hell to insane blindness. Your generation can't even begin to imagine the atmosphere surrounding the "secret vice". Rabbinical mythology proclaimed that all seed spent by men this "unnatural" way became children of demons who would all accuse their author on the Last Judgement. Etc., etc.

Masturbation neutralises tension of course, and as such can be quite useful, <u>but</u> again some degree of unsatisfied sex-tension is necessary for powering drives directed elsewhere. In other words, no tension – no potential. In other words again, there's just so much total energy available to humans, and it all depends on how they spend it what happens. Crudely put once: "If you push it through your prick you can't make it with your mind." On the other hand, if a throbbing phallus occupies the entire focal field of awareness how the hell can the poor devil think until he has settled the thing's demands? The only sensible thing to do is come to a working arrangement that if Tom Tool doesn't upset the boss's study or work periods, there will be a play session later. It's amazing how it responds similarly to toilet

76

training with a baby (same principles) "OK bowels, don't crap on carpets, that's what the bog's for."

Later on in life it can be: "OK cock, you'll get your turn in due course." Or whatever. In other words a simple conditioned reflex with a "turn-on" and "turn-off" procedure. Provided you keep the switch in your own control so that it won't work unless you say so, good enough.

The idea was to bring energies under control which would otherwise have been dissipated through sex discharges. Using conditioning procedures, no sex-demands would drain energy until granted permission via the "release symbology" chosen. The more precise and painstaking such arrangements were, the better control their constructor had. That is an interesting point for this cogent reason. Have you noticed (well who hasn't?)[42] how practically everything these days is sex-angled for sales and other purposes? Why???? We are living in a huge arena quite deliberately designed as an energy-drain through sex-levels in all directions. Once the energy is absorbed through those easy and attractive tentacles what do you suppose happens to it? For many it makes a lot of money, but it does leak away otherwise also. Millions of humans parting with actual power for what? Whom? Their own benefit? Ha ha ha Spiritual suckers the lot.

Now supposing smarter types take the trouble to fix it so that nothing operates their sexuality except signals they have set up for themselves of their own authority? They could literally walk through a wallowing world without an escape of energy anywhere until and unless they willed it themselves through whatever system of locks they had chosen. Moreover, if they had any sense they would keep their traps shut about what it was except perhaps to very close and confidential companions. Their sex or marriage partner would have to know of course.

Changes "normal topic". I've just had authors' copies of the "Magical Images" Sangreal have been working away at for the last three years. Much better than I feared at one time. In fact Bruce

---

42 Francis King told me how his manuscript on Sex Magic, accurately and learnedly entitled *Hermes and Eros* was brought out by his publisher with the cringe-making title *Sexuality, Magic and Perversion* to capture a perceived market.

Griffin the artist has made a good job of it. The designs are mainly mine, and the booklet with them I wrote.

Bloody publishers have shifted my work back to the "Spring List". In other words it's some VAT swindle of some kind of which I'll get the sticky end of course. I still wont accept their terms for "Tree of Evil". Rage and Hate!!!

Good God, its 9 pm and I haven't got anything done to speak of.

Sincerely,

Wm. G. Gray

My Dear Alan,

Thanks for your last. As a matter of fact, your reaction of depression to Grant's horrible book was about the most important. It is depressing. Why? Because it is joyless and loveless throughout, without a touch of compassion. There is neither joy nor love in real evil. You see what I mean?

Of course various people interpret the same things in different ways. They have to. All Life is One, but looks quite different at each distinct level. Have you ever tried following an identical concept all down the Tree, and working out how the same thing would come out in each sphere? An interesting exercise. You interpret Life not only as you see it, but as you live it. Who else are you entitled to interpret for?

The Theosophical notion of a "World Matreya" (Messiah) is simply their own interpretation of everyone's Inner instinct that there has to be an idealised Humano-Divine existence of some kind, and if it were focalised into incarnationary identity among Mankind, we should all be so much better for it. Of course you are too young to have known all the silly issue when the TS did try launching Krishnamurti as the Great Master. To his eternal credit he told them all to get stuffed in the politest possible way, thereby wrecking Annie Besant's ambitions altogether. One way or another, I've lost count of "World Master" rackets in my lifetime alone. They come and they go in every century. Yes, there are such things as Avatars, and damn dangerous they are for an humanity incapable of absorbing and equating their energy. One might almost say it was safer to swallow a fragment of radium. At least that would only kill a few people. How many have been murdered in the name of Jesus?

Remember the Scottish Covenanters war-cry? "The Lord Jesus – and no Quarter!" An Avatar in this age would just about blow everything apart if things went wrong.

Yes I can see that my stuff could well look pessimistic to you because of its unpromising outlooks. No spiritual pie in any sky. Just get-on-with-the-jobbism and live-life-as-it-comes. You see pessimism there where others might interpret an encouraging realism or welcome material which can actually be handled rather than romanced over. All I have ever said in effect is: "You've got to make Magic out of yourself. Nobody or anything else is going to do it for you – so – get on with the job if you want results." (I don't mean you personally here of course, but anyone at all.) No "Great Masters", no "Mighty Ones", not even God. Just you alone and what you manage to make of your relationships with "IT ALL." That is the main message of to-day, and it has to be learned one way or another, because tomorrow depends on it.

It's like realising you aren't going to win the Pools or strike rich on Ernie, and will have to work long and hard all your life for even plain bread and butter. Yet in that working you will enrich your own self with something you <u>can</u> take with you out of incarnation. How much is a million million pounds worth to a man ten seconds dead??? Remember who said: "My whole Kingdom for another minute of time."

Anyway you certainly seem to be getting the message through. Of course go into yourself and get out experiential results. Where else??? Make your own conceptions, providing you have the courage to alter or adapt them as you go along. You may think they are altering, but really it will be yourself seeing them from fresh angles. Enjoy the experience. Why not?

Oh Janay aren't bringing out my first book till the Spring List, and we are still arguing over the typefaces for the ritual of the second.

Sangreal have brought out my Magical Images at last, after two years of acrimonious correspondence. That, at least is successful. I'm spitting feathers about Janay using IBM unjustified for their printing. Just to save a few very paltry pounds. There isn't all that difference really, and unjustified margins on right make printed books look cheap and tatty no matter how well the rest is done. I'm negotiating a fourth book with Janay, but am not accepting the first terms they offered.

At the moment I'm not writing another damn thing. Not for lack of material, but from sheer "what the Hell-ness", and "end of a road" feelings. What's been said is said, now let's see what's actually done before saying any more.

One caution I will give you in a sense. Don't ever devote yourself to magic in the delusion that you will obtain fame, wealth, or other obviously tangible assets from it.[43] You won't.[44] All you'll get is led up a lifelong garden path with a deep drop at the end of it. On the other hand, if you are asking Magic to supply a means of enriching your own Identity so that at the end of a life you will be much more "Yourself" than when you entered it, then indeed you will find it has done just that for you. What more would you expect?

Anyway, best of luck in a wicked world. Let me know if you are likely to come this way. I could have a contact for you if you do. No more than that.

Something to amuse you professionally. A few weeks back I was in local hospital casualty to have a left hand injury stitched. A dear little nurse-girl of about 18 on duty. She takes down details. I give her the "trade profession or occupation" bit.

The kid looks startled. Leans close confidently and whispers under breath: "How do you spell chiro – what you said?" I whispered it back and she beamed. How do they pass exams????[45]

Bill

---

43 I did.
44 I didn't.
45 Bill was a chiropodist.

Dear Alan,

Here, have one of my spare authors' copies. Sangreal generously sent me 10. (One for each Sphere.) No, I don't want paying, it didn't cost me any money. If you ever get a book published, send me one of yours in exchange.

The booklet of course is mine. Spheres 1 and 10 my own design exclusively, the others in collaboration with Bruce Griffin. As a matter of interest, all the faces are those of living people, bar 1 and 10. No 2, for instance is Israel Regardie. No. 8, Carr Collins, and 7 his wife. 9 is a well-known psychiatrist. See if you can recognise me among them.[46] The printed descriptions are mine too. I think Bruce made a wonderful job in the end. Pity in a way I shan't be doing any more with Sangreal that I know about. My own decision.

Gawd knows what's happening about my next books. One of the Firm's chief directors has just gone in jug for five years for fraud (George Fisher), BUT, not in connection with the publishers, a phoney land-sale fiddle he was working in Spain.

£240,000 no less. There's no mention at the moment of the firm Janay folding up, but until I get some positive information I must say prospects don't look bright. It seems rather heavy-going to smash a whole company just to prevent three occult books being published. I had a letter from an agent of theirs only this Wednesday wanting to come and see me re my "TREE OF EVIL". Now of course this business has blown, I'm very chary until I see proof positive of what becomes of those contracted for already. This is a real test for the Inners. Let's see just what they are worth – or maybe not worth. It'll be interesting to see if you get a job round this way. It may be much later in the year. I've only just put the phone down from hearing that someone has found what seems to be an ideal location for a

---

46 He was the figure at Geburah.

Temple, but it will take working on. Very easy to get to from Bristol or anywhere around. So if you do come this way, I can put you in touch and you can fight your own way along with the rest for better or worse.[47]

Good Wishes.

---

47 Someone started what they hoped would be a GD temple at Turner's Tower, a small terrace in the village of Faulkland, near Bath. I never got to meet them, and the venture seems to have folded quite quickly.

Dear Alan,

Many thanks for your kindly thought about Spearman. NBG! I tried them ages ago, and he told me my stuff was too "advanced" and had not sufficient popular appeal to be profitable.

There you have the whole story. Unless big profits can be computer calculated in advance, no occult book has a chance in hell of ever reaching the public. Not a single commercial publisher will touch it. This means that in fact only popular crap is ever likely to be published again in available form. So you can take it for granted that if you want to get hold of anything I would call "genuine", you won't ever get it from modern publishing houses.

Maybe the answer is some kind of a private "subscription" publication affair, such as there used to be long ago. A number of interested parties "subscribed" to a publication, and if sufficient funds became available, the book was duly printed and brought out. All subscribers got so many copies with their names in them, and the remainder became available for general sale. Sometimes it took years getting up a subscription list. For example, Eliphas Levi's books were originally published with money his friends (including Bulwer Lytton) put up. Look how they sell now the man has been dead nearly a century.

I've just had replies from George Harrap this am. Praises my work no end but regrets not a wide enough sales likelihood as it is "limited to those already deeply involved in the occult." I never pretended otherwise.

Christ, I could write crap as well as anyone, inventing phoney "spells", "masturbation by moonlight", and all the bloody stupid irresponsible rubbish that hits the sales counters. BUT could I live with myself afterwards even if surrounded by rising royalties??? No, I'm damned if I could. And that's it. There's your story. If you want money write shit. As simple as that. Maybe some time, some place – but not in this life for sure.

Thanks a lot for the thought anyway. No kind thoughts in this world are ever wasted, even if the other kind seem so much more in evidence.

I'm sorry to say our much loved little cat died on Tuesday, so it hasn't been much of a week.

Hope to see you in summer,

Good Wishes.

Mar 26th 73

Dear Alan,

Good God, do you mean you can't get a job as a teacher <u>at all</u> <u>anywhere</u>? Or do you mean just in this district? It seems quite incredible after your training and efforts. I'm desperately sorry about that. It seems such a damned shame and waste of such valuable living-time. Or not exactly a waste, because no training is ever wasted, because it can be turned to other uses. Don't doubt it'll come in useful for something. If the worst came to the worst you could probably join one of the Forces in an Educational branch and you certainly won't be out of a job of some sort for very long. Better men have been in worse positions admittedly, but then much worse men have been in so much better positions too. Things will work out <u>of</u> <u>course</u>, but so seldom as we want.

It may interest you to know that <u>everyone</u> I know in what I vaguely call the "Western Mysteries" whose intentions are again what I call "genuine", seems to be having great opposition against their occult work at this particular period. It's more than extraordinary, it's positively evidential of an "anti-pattern" aimed against all we are trying to do in this world which may influence or affect anyone else for the better. <u>Especially</u> against whatever we might say or do which could perhaps help Individuation, or people finding their own True Selves inside them. <u>That</u> is what is being attacked in particular. That is probably why you are being inched out of teaching. You might encourage the youngsters to think for themselves instead of falling into the prepared pattern intended for them. You wouldn't believe what the relatively few genuine occultists I know have suddenly come up against fairly recently. I'm beginning to put a very unpleasant picture together, and your problem fits into the pattern too exactly to be mistaken.

I don't know if I've told you, but this bloody firm Janay are now going bankrupt, as I feared a while back, and that not only busts two of my most vital books (BOTH IN THE SELF LIBERATION AREA) but drops me down £700.00 of my money with them as well. Granted it will eventually show up as a tax-loss, but that wasn't the idea. Creditors meeting is tomorrow at Chichester, and a friend is covering it for me. I'll know more later. Make no mistake, we are up against some mighty powerful opposition, and since this world is mainly their sphere of interest, let's not underestimate it for a second, or assume that "our lot" should be able to banish all difficulties with a wave of a wand. That just isn't on in this World. Why ever do you suppose the old Occult Orders and so forth literally had to work in such secrecy, security, cover-ups, and all the rest of such inconvenience? Do you think any initiate enjoyed that or would prefer to work that way??? On the contrary, it was purely for the sake of survival on this life-level. And that's the necessity now. It hasn't changed fundamentally at all. We can survive here at the cost of some trouble and sacrifice of maybe many material gains, BUT there has to be a survival pattern. That was what I tried to outline in my now wrecked book "Self Made by Magic."

No wonder you are worried by all the news etc. That is exactly the intention behind it – to worry and depress people in general below a certain resistance level, when a psychological condition of apathy is induced. The concentration camps did it far more rapidly and drastically, but the principle behind it is the same. Get all your people into a sheep-like mass of relative unresistance until they'll take whatever crap gets hurled at them from up top. Bewilder them. In the Army it used to be said: "Bullshit baffles Brains." Break up focal points everywhere etc. The technique is very old hat, and always effective unless the bulk of people wake up to what is happening and suddenly start yelling for freedom. Not that that would help either, because a stampede panic would result in heaven knows what casualties. In fact the whole spiritual side of the situation is one God-awful bloody MESS.

So what do we do? First and foremost keep faith with our own Inner Identities. That is the "King-piece" of the problem. I know only too well it's a hell of a difficulty believing in anything worthwhile when all else is getting busted up around. How far do people believe in themselves these days? Aim all your Magic at finding your own Inner Identity. Never mind what anyone else is doing, and don't try and look for observable results on anyone else because of anything you've said or done. That's a waste of time anyway. What you do inside and with yourself WILL have effects elsewhere via the universal connections underneath so to speak. But this will take time to work out. Yet Magically, it's the only practical and sensible way, because that way one is by-passing the "opposition" altogether through Inner channels they can't touch. This may sound complicated, but it comes to the old adage that if one can't go through a wall, the only alternatives are under it, over it, or round it.

You may think you wouldn't be doing much by focalising your magical life and concentrating upon your own Inner energies. You say maybe quite fairly: "What the hell good will just one little life do in all this majority mess?" Don't judge it <u>quantitatively</u> but <u>qualitatively</u>. How big is one atomic nucleus? One microbe that decides between life and death? One thought that alters human destiny? How big would have to be one break in an electrical circuit? Work the possible in yourself, and the impossible outside it will follow later.

Now you've got two alternatives. Follow your own Inner Light of True Identity and realise you will run into difficulties materially most of your incarnation, or do the opposite and go flat out for money-power gains alone at the cost of all you once believed in. You'll succeed as this world counts success, but not a bent halfpenny can you take anywhere else, and even if your body is buried in a solid gold coffin it won't move a millimetre except towards somebody's melting pot. You could give all the money away to the poor and some other crafty bastard would get it off them again in a very little time. So what?

The chances are that most of your "occult" life, you will have to work alone – apparently.[48] Even if you find others to work with physically, it will usually break up one way or another. All the time, you will be driven back upon your own resources, and you will have to get these from the only possible supply-point – deep down inside yourself. Nowhere else. I know this sounds hard, but at least it is reliable.

Let's face it. This world is at best a very mediocre, temporary, and unsatisfactory medium for Life-experience. We have to do the best we can with what comes along, and realise that our finest and most

---

48 Absolutely right. I wonder if he 'saw' something.

developed system of living isn't in purely physical shape at all. All we can do is <u>adapt</u> ourselves as we go. What else?

Arrived with your letter was one from the original publisher Helios, asking if I had any work for consideration. Just that. I'm still coping with a sense of suspicious shock. Also an American occult group I rather like are wondering if tapes of my rituals might not sell rather well over there.[49] Something to think of. Poor old Louis Culling has died. A while back he was in such desperate straits he was living in just a tin shack on the breadline. One of the only decent "Thelemites" there were. There are endless phoney "occult" lots in the States. All very grandiose and money-oriented. In the States the "Dahlar" is GOD. Literally. You think it's like that here? You ain't seem nutting brudder. Nutting atoil.

That's about as much as I can get off just now. Let me know how things pan out. You are certainly taking them quite philosophically. Much more than I would have done at your age. Maybe we might see a bit more of you come summer.

Good luck

Bill
Hope to see a bit of you come summer.

---

49 His inners had told him that tapes of the Rollright Ritual, which he played to me when I was pissed on his whisky, would sell in large numbers. They didn't.

My Dear Alan,

You certainly have a genius for asking multi-million dollar questions on a one-cent postage stamp, as the saying goes. Vast libraries have been written about your recent query on free-will etc, and nobody is satisfied with any of the answers, least of all me.

Absolute free-will is only possible in Absolute Zoic Zero or NIL. The split-instant that point is passed into Egoic Existence, entities are committed to their Cosmic chosen courses, and have to work out their Paths of Return along whatever lines of Life they have dedicated themselves to. In ordinary consciousness you don't realise this of course. So your "free-will" is theoretically true in principle, and in the end you <u>do</u> decree your own destiny, BUT after how many Life-experiences???? In point of fact, people's "free-will" is necessarily limited to their own "Magic Circles" for the sheer sake of "Cosmic convenience" or in other words to make living together in common association mutually acceptable.

At this moment, for instance, you are technically <u>free</u> to do quite a number of things. Kill the person next to you whoever they are. Kill yourself. Smash the place up. Behave in any kind of antisocial way you want. It is equally the free-will of many others to stop you doing any of that and penalise you if you do. If you want to do anything, you have to be prepared to pay its price. If you want to fly, you must risk a crash, if travel by sea a shipwreck, or car a nasty road death, etc. Oh yes, you are free if you think the price worth paying. You know the law of Nature: "Take what you will – then pay." Nobody can get out of paying one way or another. The thing is to find – if you ever can – what in you was and yet should be your own TRUE WILL for yourself behind <u>all</u> your incarnations. Once find and align yourself with THAT, and Life will come to an automatic level. But what do you suppose we are all here for anyway? If any of us were perfect we wouldn't be here at all.

There <u>do</u> come periods and points during incarnation however, when "cross-roads" appear, and there is some choice within the overall pattern. You seem to have reached another. By and large, most of them come early in life, and later settle into "main motorways" you have to keep driving along until a let-out ramp comes along. They do, but you need to watch out not to miss one, and then evaluate whether it is worth taking anyway. Trouble is, nobody but yourself can possibly decide which is the best turn-off (if any) to take. All you can do is look for the Light-Life Line within yourself and see what seems best by it. I know this doesn't sound helpful, but what it amounts to is knowing your own Life-purpose (to some degree anyway) and firmly living to that end. That won't save you from trouble, but it will keep you on your own track, and that's what matters. For instance, you're finding your life isn't going the way you wanted with the "personality part" of you. That is, your job isn't working out, your women aren't what you'd hoped (whose are by the way?) and you can't find a wonderful Magic Group to work with that would solve all your problems for you. In other words, you are being forced by "circumstances" "Fate" or what you like, to stand up on your own spiritual feet and literally make something of yourself. What's more, you aren't doing a bad job at all – so far. You've managed in a few short years what could have taken you lifetimes otherwise, little though you realise this now. Of course it's tough, who the hell says it isn't? But it's working!

You may suppose you are alone with your Magic, but in fact you aren't. There are endless like yourself, each thinking they are the "one and only" etc etc. Yet each working along similar lines directed from where????? You don't suppose they are all going along just by sheer co-incidence do you??? You might believe it would be best if the whole lot could be organised into some world-wide affair with lots of so-called power and so forth. That's just what mustn't happen on material Life-levels. That would just about wreck the whole scheme of Individuation. Ask yourself WHY you seem "on your own". What's the purpose there? There IS one. You made it yourself before you incarnated, and now you are finding it harder to live with than it looked from those high levels. That happens to us all.

You are here in this world to make yourSELF. And furthermore in the Likeness of God Within you, in Whom you ARE. And that's it. Insofar as magic assists this process, (and it can) it's valuable to you. Outside that purpose it's no use. And you can't or shouldn't try making anybody else into what you think they ought to be for your benefit. Most of the world's troubles trace to this one way or another.

One of the main "burdens" of the Path of Initiation is exactly a sense of Inner loneliness. A kind of "out on a limb" feeling. Real Initiates make few "friends" in the accepted sense of the word. Remember they are individuating out of mass-mankind, almost as a baby leaves the warm comfort of a womb for a cold noisy, harsh, and hard uncomfortable world – until it acclimatises itself. It's a terrible feeling at first, and sometimes you have to hold on to sanity with both spiritual hands. Nothing except the tiny "Divine Spark" in yourself can possibly tell you that you are going the right way. Yet it does just that, if you hang on hard enough.

All the "pretty-pretties" of symbolical Lodge and Temple practice are really toys to teach you how to use tools. The implements of Individuation. They aren't the slightest use to anyone who hasn't the ability of using their equivalents in Inner actuality – for living with.

Remember the root of the much misunderstood word Magic is the same as "Magistery", rulership of Self, government, mastery, etc. Where does "Majesty" come from? Why a <u>Royal</u> title? What of the Blood-Royal, or Sang Real, Holy Grail etc???? Go inside yourself and get answers.

"Karma" is neither more nor less than whatever in yourself remains unequated with your own True Entity as an Individual and prevents your progress towards Universal Unity in PERFECT PEACE PROFOUND. Once equated out, it releases you that much more toward whatever Ultimate Truth may (or more likely may NOT BE). Karma is something to grow out of eventually.

Good God, I've been battling all my life with problems, and will go on so forever. So will you, tough as the assignment sounds. Try if you can, to "keep tryst" for a few moments every day with your own "Inner Self". Don't demand hard and fast answers, but let these rise naturally through the circumstances of living. You aren't as alone as you think, so learn all you can now, because the time will surely come later when you in your turn will have younger folk relying on you for some moral support in their sincere spiritual seekings. If you are honest with them, you daren't <u>demand</u> what they do, but will try and bring out what is in them to emerge. That's what they really need. You can't reasonably expect a potato to come up a cucumber.

Thesis on drug-taking.[50] Have you given enough emphasis on the deliberate suppliers of drugs for pure profit and the intentional destruction of young minds which might otherwise have done some good in this world??? Just who and what hates and despises the younger generations enough to feed them with the seeds of their own destruction??? Where is it aimed from, and why? Who encourages them so much to destroy themselves??? With what aim??? Why break up minds and souls so badly? Have you ever seen the end effects of dangerous drugs at close quarters??? Have you ever seen and experienced the tragedy of souls and minds in a state of wreckage through drug-destruction??? Have you watched and studied the smashing of a soul from start to physical finish via the poison road??? If you haven't, then your thesis is pure theory and nothing else. A broken body can die and release a soul, but a smashed soul is something that can't escape so easily. The horror and appalling tragedy of those miserably mangled lives is beyond calculation. To realise what drug addiction means, you need not theories or theses, but basics, basics, BASICS. Why. What for so deep down, and deeper than that, and deeper again. Get down till you look Hell in the face, and then – face yourself if you can.

If you go to S. California, I could give you contacts with a group there in Pasadena. But I don't know anyone in Wisconsin.

Running out of paper. Best wishes. Say how you get on.

Wm. G. Gray

---

50 As part of my final year at college. Although I was tempted to do mine on D.H. Lawrence, I finally wrote about Timothy Leary, whose *Politics of Ecstasy* seemed to be revolutionary.

Dear Alan,

The Major Arcana fit very well as I have outlined in Magical Ritual Methods. If you care to make your own attributions there's nothing to stop you, providing you have adequate basic reasons (as I had) for doing so. Undoubtedly the best are the Waite pack.

I've just signed a contract with Helios for my "TREE OF EVIL." They hope to bring it out early next year, or maybe even late this one. No news of the others yet. The police are handling the Janay debacle, and hope to get some of the cash back, but I would say this was out of the question.

Basically behind drugs is a desperate desire to escape this World because of fear. Any loophole will serve. Terrified kids kidding themselves this World can't be for real – and my God who is to throw stones at them??? It's all happened before. In the 18th century they poured raw spirits down themselves till they rotted. Now it has just got more scientifically dangerous. Any drug that gives them even a temporary "out" because life here hurts so much. In addition is the "suicide instinct" which comes automatically with a sense of overpopulation. Once people feel too many they start killing themselves one way or another, and if it can't be by war, then it has to be poison since starvation is difficult on National Assistance. They want to "lie down and die".

The people I would unhesitatingly kill without mercy of any kind are the suppliers of drugs for the sake of profit. They are deliberate killers and deserve exactly what they get. Personally I would condemn them to death by injection of their own drugs over a long period.

Regardie didn't actually support Leary in *Pentagram* at all. Gerard Noel who publishes Pentagram did a wanton bit of editing to make it look that way. He deliberately left out all Regardie's anti-drug comments. Francis never even read the article in finished form. He seldom bothers. Noel did a snide piece of jiggery pokery there. I've read the whole thing, and it reads very differently.

The root of the problem is very simple. Deliberately introduce mind-bending chemicals into the social structure until it weakens sufficiently, then take it over for exploitation. Just who and what would be most interested in wrecking Western civilisation from within for an ultimate take-over??? Not very hard to guess. Read up your Opium War history. Make people want to destroy themselves and enjoy the process.

Odd sort of summer work in mental hospitals. God help them. It is scarcely surprising minds break down or just won't stand up to the stresses of life as we are asked to accept it. You will see enough there to shake any faith you might have left in some "Ultimate Good".

So just exactly <u>what</u> "great mystical experiences" of any real value has LSD produced??? Where are any masterpieces of literature, art, or anything – engineering say – arising directly from LSD? In the Middle Ages it was ergotism caused by mouldy rye bread, and insanity abounded with it. What efficient and disciplined religious or even occult "order" makes use of hallucinogens? The Zen certainly don't, nor the Christian, nor the Tibetans. You had to learn how to work your own body-chemistry so as to make your own Inner experiences. Our bodies and their brains are <u>animals</u> that we either train properly, or ill-treat and abuse. They only last a few years anyway, and we have to make their poor brains handle types of consciousness they are barely developed enough to deal with. Eventually, after long evolution maybe, we have to learn how to live without physical bodies at all. This can't be done you think? Neither could reaching the Moon be done only thirty years back.

Haven't you twigged that keeping youngsters at school and sending them to universities and training colleges all at <u>public enormous expense</u> is only another way to hide unemployment figures??? You may live to see that day when school-leaving age is well over 20, and post graduate courses can go on till 40, then retirement at 50, so that a whole life is spent on public funds supplied by relatively few actual workers. The whole system is so bloody crooked it almost isn't true.

Pity you aren't coming this way during the summer. Let me know where you end up, and if there's anyone I know in the area worth contacting I'll see what can be done, but my contacts are relatively few these days. Best of luck.

Bill

95

25th May 73

Dear Alan,

Thanks a lot for your thought, but I'll tell you what, we'll bet a few drinks with it for the others and give them your kind regards. You would like them a lot I feel, and will probably meet up with them some time. They're a nice couple. Unexpectedly some others using my rites are coming this weekend, so we are having an unprecedentedly busy period, though its lovely to see there really <u>are</u> some worthwhile young folk like yourself still prepared to keep the Tradition of the West going. As I said they are all in threes and fours all over the place. You are not so alone as you might think. And it would be fatal to think about "getting everyone organised into one huge bunch". That's exactly what wrecks any Secret Tradition. Contacts with immediates through peripheral links are only needed to keep things going.

Look forward to seeing you later in year. No news re publishers yet.

You'll be amused to hear that Bobbie was really puzzled by the cricket ball, because she didn't twig the note you'd left under it large as life until I went and turned it over! She is rather touched actually, and means to try it with godson of 7 next time they meet up.[51]

All the best,

Wm. G. Gray

---

51 I had stayed at their place when going to my interview at Gloucester and left Bobbie (a cricket fanatic) a token gift. The godson is Marcus Claridge.

Dear Alan,

Your Million-dollar question pondered. Ultimate Infinity. Personally I think "PERFECT PEACE PROFOUND" is about the best description for Western minds accustomed to ignoring the Nil-Concept, or not realising that NIL and ALL are the unifying point of the Cosmic Circle.

To be – or not-to-be. That is the question of Life. The question of Magical – or any other kind of initiation – is HOW to "Ultimate" as WHAT.

Put crudely, do you mean (or intend, or Will) to individuate into your own Ultimate Self-state, or are you content to be simply swept along with the general tide of Life at "Cosmic convenience"? Put more crudely still, if you had the choice of being a brain-cell in the theoretical "Body of God", or a bit of the Almighty's arsehole, which would you be? Granted both bits are useful and necessary to the whole organism. But suppose you had a free choice (or Will) Which item do you feel might best be the "real you"???? Supposing you could make yourself into any bit of this Divine Corpus????? Any preferences???? Odd metaphor possibly, but the gist of it is:

A. Do you really want to do anything with yourself in Life – or
B. Don't you.

So far as Life Itself is concerned, It can use you up for anything at all, so It isn't worried particularly. The majority of humans couldn't care a sod what gets done with them so they've nothing to lose whatever, and no complaint how their spiritual assets are disposed of.

If you prefer the Individuant Path of initiation, which means no less than becoming as Eternal Entity (or the Spirit of Life) intends Itself to be through and as what amounts to your "Real Self" (as distinct from any personality, pseudo-self, etc.) then you have to bargain with Life accordingly. And Life will lean on you accordingly too! In effect It says: "Ho, so you think you're good enough to make a bit of the Real ME, do you? I hope you are, but let's find out shall we? Suppose I prod you around and read your reactions."

Magic – or any other spiritual system – simply means we are trying to evolve in order to make conscious relationships with what could be called the Direction of Cosmos. "The Gods", Whatever Name or Names you fancy.

As we evolve, those relationships become more and more matters of intention, will, judgement, and consequently more intimate and individual. That's about it, BE AS YOU WILL. All depends who (and what) "YOU" are. You, Hu, U, are all roots signifying He, That, Truth, or plain "God".

The uninstructed Westerner tends to have a horror of a Nil-concept, supposing that this means the end of them and everything. A child might as well have a horror of an Adult-concept, because it appears to mean the end of itself. Such a child would not realise that Adult-hood was an extension and expansion of itself into different Life-dimensions. Metaphorically every child has to die so that adults may live. If you ever want to be an adult, you'll have to "nullify" your childhood some time. Same if you ever intend to become more than a mere human being. You'll have to bring your species as near perfection as you can and then hop off the Tree of Life altogether into Perfect Peace Profound at Nil-point, won't you??? And don't ask how many multimillion of our years that takes, because it might equally be a split fraction of a second.

Well now, as our friend in Bath is by way of being linked loosely so to speak into fraternal ties, the correct drill is for me to give him your name and address so that he can make contact with you. Just a matter of courtesy. I've no doubt at all that he will contact you when he can. At the moment I believe he is up North with some mutual friends, but I'll drop a line when he comes back.[52]

Have just finished a little booklet on the Paths of the Tree for the Pasadena lot publishing my "Simple Guide". It doesn't look a lot on the outside, but try and find the contents anywhere else.

Good luck.

[signature]

Let me know how your Glos accommodation works out.

---

52 R.J. 'Bob' Stewart

Aug 30th 73

Dear Alan,

Thanks for your note ref change of address. You sound as if you had struck lucky.

We are having rather a full house these next two weekends, and it would be best to ring up first if you are thinking of visiting any evening.

By the way, was it you I lent a nylon raincoat to some while back??? Damned if I'm sure which person borrowed it now, but if it was you we'd appreciate it back. If not, ignore this para.

You don't seem to have empathed with our Cord for some obscure reason I'd be interested to discover, if you'd care to comment. He should be with us this weekend, so I'll have a word or so.

Did I tell you that Helios have ideas of making tape recordings (cassettes) of some of my rituals next year. Which should be interesting. Tree of Evil is being held back for New Year sales after advance publicity in New Dimensions etc. Weisers will handle in USA.

Will expect you round some evening when you can manage it.

Good wishes,

Dear Alan,

You are right, it does seem idiotic writing to Gloucester.

The Circle-Cross attributes are based on the Magical Elements of Life. For some odd reason recently, everyone seems to be buggering around with these in off-beat ways. One group shifted their Cup-Water to North – then had to move it back because it just didn't Work. Another lot moved theirs around just to be different to everyone else, and the result is a mess with walkouts.

No, the North per se is not emotion it is calculation. So what makes you think that Venus-Auriel cannot be calculating?

You can't draw a circle round in the Tree and slam the Elements of the Circle Cross as per Quarters, because although the two designs are related, their schematics are projected differently. You might as well object to Mercator's flat projection of a global design. Using the Elements, you will find on the Tree consecutively they are arranged in balanced opposites, i.e.:

Tiph-Yesod	Fire-Water
Netzach-Hod	Earth-Air

The Tree itself is an arrangement of balanced opposites, so that is how things work out on it. The Circle-Cross is a scheme of concentric successives. So that is how the same factors are arranged thereon. How do you convert Time into Space and make Events?

Strictly speaking, there isn't a North and South Pole to this world at all. Both poles are North-Arctic, and the Equator is South to both. Factually we have:

Poles.	Point of least movement of globe.	North.
Equator.	Point of most movement of globe.	South.
Rotation rising point of sun.		East.
Rotation setting point of sun.		West.

If you work those round you will find NSEW (or whichever you start with in that order) does work out as the Tree has them.

Auriel means the Light of God. That is the Light in Darkness. Which is not only the North Star, but <u>also</u> Venus which is the Morning and Evening "star" of approaching and disappearing darkness. Light over darkness of the Earth.

If none of that is any help, then the only thing to do is work out your own attributions and live them yourself, or write a book proving how much everything is up the creek and what ought to take its place. It should make interesting reading. I'd love a copy when it comes out.

Small job for you if you've time. Check out an SPCK (Society for the Promotion of Christian Knowledge) shop in Gloucester, address, 28 Westgate St, and see if they still sell incense charcoal blocks, or/and "Glastonbury" incense. The other SPCK shops do, but I'm getting tired of having it from Bristol.

I think Bob Stewart is a bit fed up with waiting to meet you and has rather written you off. You may run into him at the folk club one time, but he doesn't do Gloucester very often now, and very rarely Cheltenham indeed. I see him at intervals otherwise.

Good wishes,

June 10th 1974

Dear Alan Richardson,

Thank you for a copy of your little book published by Thorsons.[53]

Though, as you say yourself, it is scarcely original, it does have the merit of being sincere and I believe it may indeed be of help to young and inexperienced folk who are seeking something a little more solid than they have bought at the expense of effort and money maybe sacrificed for very inadequate returns. It can certainly do no harm that I know of.

May I wish you good luck in USA?

Yours sincerely

Wm. G. Gray.

---

53 *An Introduction to the Mystical Qabalah.*

An Holy Hiatus

Alan Richardson

'Holy Hiatus' is a typically William G. Gray term. As the purpose of this book is to show how a sort of Magical Apprenticeship was worked out through Bill's letters, I don't need to go into details about the decay of our relationship during my dreadful time in Gloucester; which was paralleled by the decay of yet another relationship with a girl back in Newcastle. This was why I couldn't 'empath' with his Cord: I was hanging on for dear life.

I was never much good at wielding a wand in a Circle, but – ye gods – you could never teach me much about wearing my heart on my sleeve and going around in spirals.

During my time in Gloucester I visited Bill numerous times but never sought to join his group, adored his wife Bobbie, and saw many examples of her husband's formidable clairvoyance. It was through the encouragement of the latter that I managed to wangle myself a somewhat phoney scholarship to the University of Kentucky, funded by Sir Ernest Kleinwort. This was where, Bill predicted, I'd meet a woman who would give me TROUBLE – as he might have written it. Long story, not relevant here, but with archetypal echoes outlined in my *Earth God Risen*.

On the final visit during that first phase of our relationship I had had a dreadful day in the classroom, one lesson ending with several boys calling out *Cunt Cunt Cunt* – and I was too weak to do anything. Although, to be kinder to myself, I did find out in the US that I had a tumour within my ear which had been responsible for all sorts of torments. During that last visit to Bennington Street, however, I wore my misery like a huge cloak. Norman Gibbs came in and was startled. They both sort of cut me dead and talked over my head. Bobbie was kind and maternal to me. As I left, Bill refused to give me his usual semi-Masonic handshake and told me that in my present state I would be a menace – he hissed the word – to any worthwhile magical group.

And he was right.

Yet I never gave up with Magic – or it never gave up with me. Bill was right: once you start, you can never go back. I wrote and wrote and wrote – but almost nothing got accepted. Thank god it didn't, because it was crap. For some reason, probably just looking for an excuse to maintain contact with him, however tenuous, I sent him another query from the States, added some babbling in which I manfully accepted the fact that he didn't like me, and included International Reply Coupons in lieu of an SAE. The following is his reply…

Aug 7th. 75

Dear Alan Richardson,

Your letter and reply coupons received. So far as I know, you, or anyone is perfectly entitled to use the Tarot-Tree system as outlined in my books. It is usually considered courteous in literary circles to make a brief reference to source if known. The only place copyright applies is if more than fifty words of someone else's work is quoted. Seemingly one can quote up to that number without any worries.

You might also care to mention the TALKING TREE, printed by Weisers of New York this year sometime, which deals a great deal with the Tarot-Path system.

You seem to be attributing your own feelings about yourself on one level, to me on another, which is quite a common process of consciousness-transference. In other words you are using your image of me to raise reactions in your psyche. No reason at all why you shouldn't, providing you realise what you are doing. Otherwise you will make a lot of quite unnecessary and superfluous worry and annoyance for yourself and nobody else.

Neither I, nor anyone I know of, dislikes you. That would be to imply personal feelings which were not involved. If you failed to harmonise with us, then that is our loss as much as yours. It does not mean that you will not harmonise with others who will consider you a very wonderful soul, look to you for leadership, and place you very much on a pedestal. You may yet be hailed as the most amazing young writer of occult works ever read in USA. There may be a glowing and glorious future ahead of you in America. Why not? You would certainly be well advised to stay there if you can and make use of opportunities. All you have to do is always tell people what they want to hear, and never what they need to know. That is the whole secret in a nutshell.

You write of "severed links" and "reconciliation" as if I had expelled you from something – or thereabouts, or quarrelled with you in some way. I was not aware of doing more than quietly close a door there was no point in holding open any longer. There are millions of other doors which will open widely in welcome for you, so you need not trouble about one single shut entrance in the slightest. Write it off and forget it. Maybe there was nothing worth your while on the other side anyhow. Never bother what anyone thinks of you – think truly of yourself.

Wm. G. Gray.

Final Bit

Alan Richardson

When I took up with him again in 1983 I was no longer an unformed youth. In the interim I had crossed some sort of abyss and found my own Inner sources of inspiration, and this was obvious to him. I still adored Bobbie. Thence followed a whole new series of letters from Bill, all embossed with his new symbol, all written in his wonderfully curmudgeonly style. Clearly he had been busy in the meantime too and had found his Holy Grail – though his Sangreal Sodality never interested me one bit. I knew by then that I never wanted or needed to join any kind of group and disliked talking about Magic even with magicians. In my first letter to him after several years I asked about Dion Fortune (whom he had met on outer and inner levels), the Society of the Inner Light, which he continued to blast, and a very important figure in the orbit of both called Colonel Seymour. The remaining content of his long letter is not relevant to the present book, but here is the first and entirely typical portion of his reply...

14 Bennington St
Cheltenham
Glos GL50 4ED

18 April 1983

Dear Alan

Nice to hear from you after all this time. Last I remember you sent me a very sad note implying that you were all washed up and I'd never hear from you again. You may not remember it, but you did. And here you turn up again all bouncy with a string of writings to your name. Good for you!

Sorry but I can't help you at all, but I would if I could. I've never even heard of Seymour, let alone met him, and I couldn't care less about the guy anyhow…

Wm. G. Gray

Appendix

Bill told me that Carr Collins, his rich financial sponsor in the States, was completely unable to understand even the most basic concepts of the Kabbalah. So he wrote for him what he termed his 'Simple-simple Guide to the Tree of Life.' One evening he read out large portions of this to me with great delight, with the air of a scholar who has just realised he could write children's stories. I do not know if it ever got published.

And although I have no interest in the Kabbalah today, below is my own simple-simple guide to help explain some of the concepts that imbued his letters to me, when I was 'building the Tree' in my young aura on a daily basis.

* * *

The Kabbalah can also be spelled: Qabalah, Cabala, or simply QBL – there are no vowels in Hebrew. In fact the name is derived from the root word 'Qibel', meaning 'to receive', which is sometimes also written as *k-b-l (kuf-beit-lamed)*. This refers to secret oral teachings, passed on from one initiate to the next, through generation after generation. Although the origins are Hebrew, it has been altered (purists might say debased) and developed (some might say corrupted) to such an extent that it forms the foundation stone of the Western Esoteric Tradition. Almost every Western spiritual system in modern times can trace its origins to the single glyph known as the Kabbalistic *otz chaim*, or Tree of Life.

It was an esoteric doctrine passed on from initiate to initiate, a mystic lore that was said to be capable of explaining the secrets of the heavens above and the earth beneath. Its main books were the *Sepher Yetzirah*, or 'Book of Creation', and the *Zohar*, or 'Book of Splendour', which was written in Spain by Moses de Leon in the 13th Century.

The theoretical Kabbalah contains elements from ancient Egyptian, Babylonian and Greek philosophies, spiced up with the mysticism of Philo and the early Christian Gnostics, with the doctrines of reincarnation, transmigration, and the enduring realities of Good and Evil, Light and Darkness thrown into the mix.

If the theoretical Kabbalah proved irresistible to the mystics, then the practical Kabbalah proved itself a manna to the magicians. And it is that diagram known as the *Otz Chaim*, or Tree of Life, which provided the framework upon which all else was hung. One commentator described it as the 'Mighty and All-embracing glyph of the Universe and the soul of Man.' Surprisingly, despite the bombast, it is exactly that. Crowley wrote in the Introduction to the *Liber 777* that the all-important Tree-glyph is:

> ... the skeleton on which this body of truth is built. The juxtaposition and proportion of its parts should be fully studied. Practice alone will enable the student to determine how far an analogy may be followed out. Again, some analogies may escape a superficial study. The Beetle is only connected with the sign Pisces through the Tarot Trump The Moon. The Camel is only connected with the High Priestess through the letter Gimel.
>
> Since all things whatsoever (including no thing) may be placed upon the Tree of Life, the Table could never be complete. It is already somewhat unwieldy; we have tried to confine ourselves as far as possible to lists of Things Generally Unknown.

This is an instance in which his scholarship confuses – and is meant to confuse. It is also an instance in which obscurity is taken for profundity. While not wanting to throw the Crowleyan moon-child out with the Aeon's bathwater, readers must be bold enough to make their own Correspondences, using his as interesting but not necessarily infallible examples. As we have noted, much of *777* was simply cribbed from the work done by Mathers, who spent endless hours of unpaid work in the Reading Room of the British Museum, translating and writing and bringing a New Age into existence with the help of his fey wife Moina.

Crowley goes on to explain:

> Many columns will seem to the majority of people to consist of mere lists of senseless words. Practice, and advance in the magical or mystical path, will enable little by little to interpret more and more.

Even as a flower unfolds beneath the ardent kisses of the Sun, so will this table reveal its glories to the dazzling eye of illumination.[54]

The Master Therion, to give him one of his many Magical Names, was a very young 34 when he wrote this. As Carl Jung once commented, when the archetypes (i.e. gods) first start to speak, they are *always* pompous. And as the *enfant terrible* of the occult world, Crowley could certainly be that.

A simplified image of the Tree is:

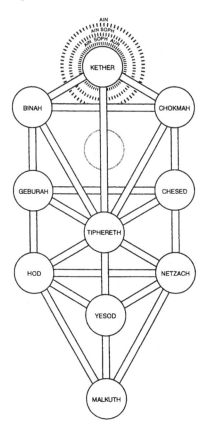

According to the revelation, all life proceeded via a series of emanations beginning from the *Ain*. This is complete void and vacuum. Not simply 'nothing', but not even the existence of 'nothing' itself – absolute and incomprehensible. Then came *Ain Soph*. If *Ain*

---

54 *Liber 777*, Aleister Crowley 1908.

is the *idea* of infinity, then *Ain Soph is* infinity. For convenience, *Ain Soph* is the Waters. Then *Ain Soph* 'moved' and created the Limitless Light known as *Ain Soph Aur.*

From the limitless ocean of that Absolute Nothingness came the single point of pure and condensed white light known as Kether, which is that state of consciousness that we might crudely (very crudely) describe as God.

It was from this first sphere, or *sephirah*, that the universe began to manifest itself in the numerical sequence shown, so that Kether (1) is at the level of absolute spirit, and Malkuth (10) is the realm of densest matter. It is in Malkuth, the earth-sphere, that we find ourselves. The Tree provides us with a ladder by which we can attempt to climb back up to our Source.

The spheres themselves are clearly arranged on three columns known as Pillars. All the positive, upbuilding energies in the universe are linked with the right-hand column, and all the negative, breaking-down forces placed on the left. In this sense, however, 'negative' was never regarded as evil in itself, any more than it is evil to knock down buildings (or psychological edifices) which are dangerously decayed. It is wrong to associate Good with Positive and Evil with Negative. Being always positive, always saying 'yes,' can create just as much evil within the world as its unbalanced opposite. The balance, then, is represented by the middle pillar.

Within these columns we can resolve the universe for ourselves, if we are uncompromising enough: Yes/No/Maybe, White/Black/Grey. Sometimes, as all magicians know, the best way to deal with the world is to retreat into the basics, and nothing else.

By analysing the spheres, however, we can add some subtleties to the way that these three qualities express themselves.

We can best imagine the Tree as a kind of filing system which is divided into ten compartments, and into which everything – *everything* – can be placed. Our initial problem is simply that of having the exact nature of this system explained to us, because after that it begins to explain itself.

Had there been 26 compartments then this would present no problem at all, for it would be based upon the alphabet. Into the compartment 'L' for example, would go leopards, lemurs, light, locusts and love. While it would be simplicity itself to store such data the exercise would be meaningless on any spiritual level: it is no good looking for love and finding lice, lugworms and loquaciousness. But with the system used by the Tree we can not only store away our own experiences in a particular area – intellectual, emotional or spiritual – but we can use to it to lead us on into the collective experience of mankind as a whole.

Each of the spheres upon the Tree has some basic attributions. So do the paths linking them.

Sphere	Archangel	Divine Name	Colour	Magical Image
Kether	Metatron	Eheieh	Brilliance	Face of an Old Man, in profile
Chokmah	Ratziel	Jehovah	Brilliance	Masculine bearded face, full-on
Binah	Tzaphkiel	Jehovah Elohim	Blackness	A mature woman
Chesed	Tsadkiel	El	Blue	A wise king, on his throne
Geburah	Khamael	Elohim Gibor	Red	A warrior king, on his chariot
Tiphereth	Michael	Jehovah Eloah va Daath	Rose-pink	A child, priest-king, sacrificed god.
Netzach	Auriel	JHVH Tzavoos	Emerald	Beautiful naked woman
Hod	Raphael	Elohim Tzavoos	Orange	An hermaphrodite
Yesod	Gabriel	Shadai el Chai	Violet	Naked man, very strong
Malkuth	Sandalphon	Adonai ha Aretz	Olive	Mother Nature, on her throne

To understand how we can use each of these as keys into areas of consciousness, we need to look at each one in sequence.

KETHER

The Crown. The Point within the Circle. Instead of visualising God as some omnipotent deity in human form, visualise him as an all-pervasive radiance, underlying all and everything. Then go a stage further and imagine that light concentrating itself into an intense pinpoint which hangs within the absolute nothingness and complete blackness of the unmanifest universe, before The Beginning. This, then, is Kether: a pinpoint of pure white light which contains All. This is the universe before the Big Bang. This is the Essence.

CHOKMAH

Wisdom. When Kether became aware of itself it exploded outward in what we might describe as the first Cosmic Laugh. This is Chokmah, which represents the archetypal male and is the sphere of all the outrushing, thrusting and forceful energies as they emerge from the Source. One of its images is that of an upright pole, which should speak for itself in phallic terms. All phallic symbolism, therefore, can find an ultimate placement in this second sphere.

BINAH

Understanding. If Chokmah is the sphere of pure and dynamic *force* on archetypal levels, then Binah balances it with the archetype female qualities of pure and receptive *form*. It is the sphere associated with the black-robed Great Mother, the planet Saturn, and that revelation known as Sorrow, in its spiritual sense: 'All life is suffering' as Buddha said, but through that (through Binah) we can begin to understand the deepest parts of life's mystery.

These three spheres are known as the Supernal Triad. They represent the innermost essence of all that we find in denser levels of manifestation. All of us have qualities of positive and negative within us. How we use these qualities, as opposed to over-indulging in them, determines how much Wisdom (Chokmah) or Understanding (Binah) we have. It is nothing to do with what sex a person may be. Men can be Binah figures just as women can relate to Chokmah.

CHESED

Mercy. The planet is Jupiter. It is the sphere of benevolence, generosity, philanthropy, and all those energies which go toward the creation of stable, peaceful civilisations.

GEBURAH

Justice. Its planet being Mars, it is the natural balance to the sphere of Chesed. It is that energy which ensures that anything effete, corrupt and putrid (however this manifests) is regularly scoured, purified, or swept away completely. Although its traditional symbol is that of the pentagram, the modern image of a surgeon's knife is more indicative.

TIPHERETH

Beauty. Both Chesed and Geburah resolve themselves within Tiphereth, the sphere of the Sun. It is the sphere of all those Sacrificed Gods who abound in major religions, and who bring harmony to the world by dying for our sakes. Harmony is, in fact, one of its titles. Not the placid and often pathetic harmony of, say, an English vicar, but the harmony achieved by the nuclear forces reacting with the Sun itself, with its power to heal or destroy depending upon where we are placed at the time.

This trinity of Chesed/Geburah/Tiphereth is known as the Ethical triad. They represent those qualities which lift us above mere self-absorption toward a consideration of life and humanity as a whole.

NETZACH

Victory, or *Achievement.* This is the sphere of Venus, with all those quickening impulses which might loosely be termed 'romantic,' and find expression in the arts generally and in our emotional behaviour personally.

HOD

Glory, or *Splendour.* This is the sphere of Mercury, whose qualities of pure intellect neatly balance the raw emotion of Netzach, and which find expression every time we act rationally, and logically, or indulge ourselves in the sciences.

YESOD

Foundation. The place of the Moon, and the unconscious mind, and what we might think of as the instincts upon which so much of our existence depends. It is also the realm of the astral plane, the 'treasure-house of images,' and because of the use made of this by magicians, this particular trinity of Netzach/Hod/Yesod is known as the Magical Triad.

MALKUTH

Kingdom. The material world on which we all live and find expression. All of the above spheres "pour down" into it. Malkuth contains them just as our physical body contains our mind, soul and spirit. It is related to the four elements of Earth, Water, Air and Fire, which we might think of as Solids, Liquids, Gases and Radiations.

There is an eleventh sphere also, known as DAATH, or Knowledge, where Malkuth used to be before the 'Fall', but that needn't concern us here.

As we can see from the diagram, the spheres of the Tree are joined by paths, which might be regarded as the blending points. Thus the path between Yesod and Netzach represents that area within our consciousness which rises from pure blind instinct and leads into the glow of more romantic considerations: where having sex turns into making love. Or else we can study that path connecting Hod and Netzach and make the careful balance that we must all strike sometimes between soulless intellect and brainless passion.

So we can begin to see how this unique filing system of the Tree of Life can work. Like a novice secretary, the neophyte will handle the system clumsily at first, often putting things into the wrong holes; but with rapidly increasing assurance the peculiar patterns and interrelationships between the spheres will begin to teach of their own accord.

For example, all those gods related to the intellectual 'Hermetic' arts would be equated with the sphere of Hod: Thoth, Hermes, Merlin, etc, while all those figures of romance and enchantment will go into Netzach: Nimuë, Nephthys, Freya and so on.

There is no dogma attached to this (or there shouldn't be): militant feminists are quite welcome to reverse the polarities and adapt them to their own peculiar vision of the universe. As long as the neophyte makes his or her own efforts in determining the Correspondences for each sphere, that process known as 'Building the Tree in the Aura' will take place. It is when this happens that the filing system starts to become more akin to a super-computer of spiritual possibility.

The forces on the Tree are all perfectly balanced with one another. It is impossible to 'trick' these energies into giving something for nothing. There are always prices to be paid, harmonies which will be maintained. And when the Tree is built into the aura it becomes a device which enables us to connect our own limited consciousness with the unlimited consciousness of the universe. Whatever changes we affect within ourselves ultimately affect the whole of existence. We become part of the great cosmic balancing act and must accept a grave responsibility for an inward kind of decency and honesty.

But in purely magical terms it means that in time, the magician will be able to pick up one symbol – an *ankh* for example – and that single glyph will give him access not only to the huge store of his own ideas, but also to the infinite experience of the collective unconscious. By lifting this simple device from the altar of his conscious mind, with ritualistic intent, he is potentially in touch with the experience of every Egyptian worshipper of Isis, every latter-day hippie, every astrologer who has ever marvelled at Venus, and every Roman who has ever adored that goddess as she rose from the sea. It becomes simpler with practice: like driving a car, or handling complex machinery, it becomes almost automatic. In time, you can forget about it all with your conscious mind because it propels you inward from unconscious levels. And then, as so many other magicians have learned to do, you can sit down in some quiet place, summon up your gods, goddesses or guides, and start to perform real magic…

The **Four Worlds** of manifestation can also be seen in the structure of the Tree.

Kether	Atziluth (Emanation)
Chokmah/Binah	Briah (Creation)
Chesed/Geburah Tiphereth Netzach/Yesod	Yetzirah (Formation)
Malkuth	Assiah (Action)

They can also be seen within each of the Sephiroth, 'descending' the Tree:

	Atziluth	Briah	Yetzirah	Assiah
	Divine Name	*Archangel*	*Angelic Choir*	*Material World*
Kether	Eheieh	Metatron	Chioth ha Qodesh	Primum Mobile
Chokmah	Yahweh	Ratziel	Auphanim	Zodiac
Binah	Yahweh Elohim	Tzaphkiel	Aralim	Saturn
Chesed	El	Tzadkiel	Chasmalim	Jupiter
Geburah	Elohim Gibor	Khamael	Seraphim	Mars
Tiphereth	Yahweh Eloah ve Daath	Mikael	Malakim	Sun
Netzach	Yahweh Tzabaoth	Auriel	Elohim	Venus
Hod	Elohim Tzabaoth	Raphael	Beni Elohim	Mercury
Yesod	Shaddai el Chai	Gabriel	Ashim	Moon
Malkuth	Adonai ha Aretz	Sandalphon	Kerubim	Earth

William Gray's insights diverged somewhat from the traditional Golden Dawn attributions.[55]

Number	Sephirah	Type of consciousness	
0	Nil	The Unconscious	(I AM NOT)
1	Summit	Being	(The I AM)
2	Wisdom	Knowing	(This from That)
3	Understanding	Feeling	(I and They)
4	Compassion	Attraction	(loving, wanting)
5	Severity	Repulsion	(hating, rejecting)
6	Beauty	Stabilising	(equanimity, normality)
7	Victory	Increasing	(gaining amount of awareness)
8	Glory	Improving	(quality gain of awareness)
9	Foundation	Constructing	(arrangement of awareness)
10	Kingdom	Continuity	(memory)

---

55 *Magical Ritual Methods*, William G. Gray. Helios 1969.

To which can also be added the vowel sonics for use with the Elements. These are what might be thought of glamorously as the 'Names of Power'. Instead of the Hebrew god-names for each Quarter, Gray suggests that by using these simple vowel sounds, at the same time as meditating upon the Archangels and Attributes of the Quarters, a great deal of energy can be invoked.

EAST	EEEEEEEEEEEEEEEEEEEE (toning to EI)
SOUTH	IIIIIIIIIIIIIIIIIIIIIIIIIIIIIIIIIIIIIII (toning to IO)
WEST	OOOOOOOOOOOOOOOOOO (toning to OA)
NORTH	AAAAAAAAAAAAAAAAAA (toning to AE)

So the Kabbalah as used by the magicians of the West is not a religion. It is more akin to an infinitely flexible, self-programmable computer that will enable you to rearrange and file the entirety of your experience, and find out things you never knew were lurking inside of yourself.

CPSIA information can be obtained
at www.ICGtesting.com
Printed in the USA
BVHW070251151220
595602BV00008B/535